FINANCIAL ETHICS

FINANCIAL ETHICS

by

Andrew M. McCosh

The University of Edinburgh
Scotland, UK

Kluwer Academic Publishers
Boston/Dordrecht/London

Distributors for North, Central and South America:
Kluwer Academic Publishers
101 Philip Drive
Assinippi Park
Norwell, Massachusetts 02061 USA
Telephone (781) 871-6600
Fax (781) 871-6528
E-Mail <kluwer@wkap.com>

Distributors for all other countries:
Kluwer Academic Publishers Group
Distribution Centre
Post Office Box 322
3300 AH Dordrecht, THE NETHERLANDS
Telephone 31 78 6392 392
Fax 31 78 6546 474
E-Mail <orderdept@wkap.nl>

 Electronic Services <http://www.wkap.nl>

Library of Congress Cataloging-in-Publication Data
McCosh, Andrew M.
    Financial ethics / by Andrew M. McCosh.
    p. cm.
  Includes bibliographical references and index.
  ISBN 0-7923-8556 - X
  1. Finance - - Religious aspects. 2. Finance - - Moral and ethical
aspects. 3. Capital market - - Moral and ethical aspects. I. Title.
  HG103 .M37 1999
  332 - - dc21
                                                      99-37164
                                                        CIP

Printed on acid-free paper.

Printed in the United States of America

DEDICATION

to Anne

I acknowledge with gratitude the valuable discussions I have had with Robin Downie, Francis McHugh, Larry Rasmussen, Don Shriver, and most especially with Joseph Houston during the preparation of this volume.

- Andrew M. McCosh

TABLE OF CONTENTS

PART III - TESTING, AND THEN MARKETING, THE SECOND ETHICAL COMMAND

PREFACE

The global capital markets affect all of us. Those who work in the markets are affected most, of course, but we are all affected, at least in terms of our material welfare, by what these markets do. The markets have grown very considerably over the last thirty years. This growth has created an expectation of further growth, and there is great pressure on the capital markets workers to continue to "perform". These workers have a long history of operating in a very ethical fashion, and of dealing firmly with those few workers who have deviated. The growth in pressure to perform is a force which acts against the continued maintenance of these high standards. Ethics is one of the lifelines that protect the capital market workers from the temptation to cut corners. We will consider those ethical commands which flow from religious sources, and their implications for capital market workers.

We collate the instructions of the founders and early leaders of the religions concerning business, with particular reference to finance. Judaism, Islam, Buddhism and Christianity are all quite similar in what they require of the business financier. A set of thirteen topics are found to be common ground between the four religions. Of these, the majority are already almost universally practiced within the financial industries, and these maxims do not need any additional work beyond their maintenance. There are, however, two instructions from the religions to the financial community and which have not as yet been obeyed.

The first command is that the financial community should take steps to fund improved systems for food distribution to the poorest sections of the poorest countries. They should use their considerable ingenuity to make such funding profitable as well as effective. The second command states that a financier does not have the right to deprive anyone of the probability of a livelihood without procuring the provision of adequate compensation. Six tools for implementing the second command are reviewed. These are prayer, training, an approach involving the creation of an ethical impact report, a new set of financial instruments which would diminish the number and intensity of capital market disputes, a changed system for rewarding financiers, and law. The discussion concludes that the first four of these are worth pursuing.

<u>Introduction</u>
The task of moving resources from where they are to where they are needed, transforming them during the movement perhaps, and making this movement expeditiously, is, on a global scale, a monstrously complex job. No human could do it. Several, such as Mao Tse Tung and Stalin, have tried, but all they have managed is to prove it cannot be done. It requires the active intervention of millions of people to get resources shifted around the world with minimum wastage and loss. The world's trading systems and markets serve as focal points through which each of these market workers can interact with the remainder, so that the resource, whatever it may be, is moved, processed, or transformed. The capitalist system of resource management depends on these markets, and upon the people who work in these markets, to fulfil the mission. In searching for a profitable trade, the market workers will try out new approaches, new agreements, new locations, and new ideas. Most of these will fail, but the successes will be generally adopted to the betterment of the entire system.

Over the last few decades, many of the world's markets have become huge in scale, and operate at far faster speeds than ever before. There has been more trade, the trade is more global in scope, and the communications systems have speeded up to an instantaneous level. One consequence of these escalations is that the market workers are subject to greater pressure to perform than was true in years gone by. Nowhere is this pressure to perform felt more acutely than in the markets for money in all its forms.

There are many ways people can react to pressure. Some people lap it up. Others flee. Still others collapse. Most just cope, somehow, usually by making the whole task a bit simpler, if that is possible, and by focussing on the essentials. For a worker in the capital markets, the essentials are making a living through profitable trading and conforming to the regulations governing the market. Being ethical is essential too, in the sense of conforming to the instructions in the company ethics manual. Being ethical in the sense that most ethicists and theologians use the word is not essential, except by coincidence.

This book is an exploration of the relatively new subject of financial ethics. I am separating business ethics from financial ethics, though there are obvious points of contact. Most of the writings on business ethics are concerned with the direct contact between the business person and another person, and how the former should behave during this contact. In the case of financial ethics, the problem is more distant, more amorphous, less immediate, but has the potential to be more damaging. When a finance person acts, he makes it possible for another business person to take an action which may have ethical consequences. This book rejects the idea that the finance person is exempt from consideration of these ethical consequences. This book takes the view that, in certain circumstances and up to a point, a finance person can be unethical at one remove.

In this book we will follow two different trails, which will eventually be brought together. The whole process is illustrated in diagram one on the next page. The first trail is an exploration in chapters one and two of the general nature of the finance industry, of the institutions which make it up, of the people in it and the pressures they are under. The first trail also examines the nature of the reward system in the finance industry, and uses the work of Steven Kerr to forecast how the rewarded people will behave. We will also take a look at one idea of Milton Friedman's, and will dispute it. We will contend that the speed with which the finance industry now operates makes it essential that the financiers and the business people build the ethical considerations in at the outset of a venture; there won't be time to do that later.

The second trail is an examination of the guidance we can obtain from four of the world's great religions on exactly how we ought to behave when we are engaged in the financial industry. This second part of the book is contained in chapters three to seven. If we propose to advise the financiers to be ethical, it is important to know what we mean by that, and to call upon reliable sources in putting the definitions together. Chapter three explains why we are using religious sources and why we are using the four particular religions chosen. The next four chapters extract business and financial commands from the source documents and one or two important interpretive writings of Judaism, Christianity, Islam, and Buddhism.

Part three of the book is a distillation of the concepts from the religions, an application of the concepts to the modern financial world, and a discussion of the various organisational tools which might be used to put them into operation. It was slightly surprising to find how similar the source books of the main religions were in respect of their business instructions.

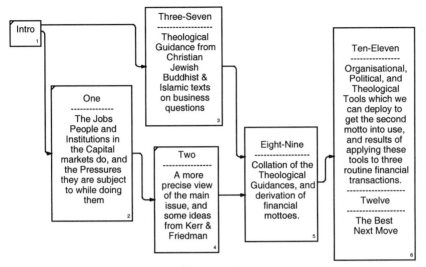

Diagram One:- The Outline of this Book

The religions vary massively on other topics, but they were close to unanimous about how business and trade should be carried on. The distillation of the commands of the religions is given in chapter eight, and an interpretation of these in the language of modern finance is developed in chapter nine.

It is important to note that many of the business and financial commands issued by the religious leaders and founders have become so much second nature to us that we do not really need to be told about them again. Some of the rest are well catered for in the law of every advanced country. There are exactly two ethical commands which are supported by all four religions and which are not second nature to us and which are not part of the law of the advanced countries.

"Ethical Command One" relates to the need to engage in financing the distribution of food to the poorest communities and the prohibition of financing the hoarding of essential goods. This one was completely unexpected. This is a very major ethical command, which has been derived from the first principles of the four religions. I had not the slightest previous inkling that this ethical command was going to be one of the results. It is clear that the financial and business sectors have given close attention to the tasks of food distribution within the developed world, and that they have joined with charities and supra-governmental organisations to try to address the matter in the least developed countries. Unfortunately, this task, within the LDCs, has not been as successful as everyone would have wished. There have been a number of important meetings, at which financial institutions have tried to work out how to deal with one financial part of this issue, the job of linking the microlenders to the global financial system. This will be considered again later, but in less detail than the other ethical command.

The other major ethical command to the financial industry from the four religions, is that they should not finance a project which will deprive someone of the probability of making a livelihood without also procuring the financing of adequate compensation. The derivation of this, "Ethical Command Two", from the first principles of the religions is shown in chapter nine.

Chapters ten, eleven, and twelve constitute part three of the book. Chapter ten sets up three "test cases" in the financial industry, and discusses them from a purely financial or economic viewpoint. They have been chosen simply as examples of the sorts of things that financiers do every working day. The goal is to see whether the two commands, and especially ethical command two, would bring about any change in normal practice in handling these test case transactions. Chapter eleven is a lengthy analysis of the various organisational tools which might be employed to try to put ethical command two into operation, and this chapter also assesses the chance that each tool would work.

The tools are quite different from each other and independent of each other. It would be possible, at least in theory, to apply all of them. The tools are prayer, mind expansion and training, new capital instruments, ethical impact statements, new reward structures, and changed laws. Chapter eleven is devoted to trying out each tool on each of the three test cases to see what might be expected to happen.

Chapter twelve is the conclusion, and there is also an epilogue which sets forth a plan for future action by the present author. I want to take this exploration further, and it seems reasonable to base the next few steps on the results already obtained. The best next move may not be feasible; the second best next move may be all I can expect to handle. At the same time, it would be a significant step forward in developing the new intellectual subject of financial ethics if Ethical Command Two could be put into the literature for assessment and evaluation. It would be even better if I could get some of the finance community to take positive action on Ethical Commands One and Two. That would not only be a signal of success for the project, it would also be a valuable step towards relieving the pressure on the client population of the financial communities, and therefore towards relieving the pressure on the financial communities themselves

Part One - The Problem Domain

Chapter One:- The Jobs of the Capital Markets, and the People who Do Them

This part sets the scene for the study of capital markets. Within the part, this chapter describes some people and their jobs. The overall goal of the project is to establish that there is serious pressure on capital market people to under-consider ethical issues, and to find some ways of alleviating that problem. Before we can do that, some readers who are not involved in the operations of the capital markets might welcome a discourse of modest length on what the capital markets actually do, and how they do it. Readers who are familiar with the capital markets may wish to check that my description of their situation is correct (though I readily accept that they may find it over-simplified), or may prefer to skip forward to page 29, where the problem definition part begins.

Most people, when the word "market" comes up, think in terms of a series of rows of stalls, set out on a Saturday morning perhaps, to which a number of the local farmers bring their produce, some of the arts and crafts people bring hand-made brushes and furniture, and other stalls offer clothing, cats, catfood, dogs, dogfood, various other animals, dishes, and a host of other offerings. The object of the market is to provide a forum where the people who want to sell something know they have a good chance of being able to sell it, and the people who have a need know that they they may be able to fulfil it, or at worst have a pleasant outing. I hope that readers of this will never let go of that image of a market as our discussion of capital markets proceeds. Capital markets look different from the Saturday market, they smell different, they sound different, but they are the same in essence. Somebody is trying to sell something, and somebody else is there because they think they may want to buy something. The only important difference is that the "something" in the capital markets is a contract denominated in money. It may be present money or future money, it may be certain money or only likely money, it may involve a myriad of other rights and obligations as well as money, but it will surely be a contract involving money, in one or more of its ten thousand different contractual forms.

Almost everyone has interacted with the capital markets, at least in their retail manifestation. Borrowing money from a building society (or a Savings and Loan) to buy a house involves exchanging a promise to make a lengthy series of payments in local currency in exchange for having the society make a single very large payment on the borrowers' behalf now. Borrowing from a credit card company to buy a holiday or a consumer durable involves a similar promise, though the series of payments is usually much briefer. Buying Cyprus pounds for a holiday trip usually requires the immediate payment of our home currency, and incidentally entails an interaction with a bank or with an exchange bureau. Salary earners are accustomed to the concept that there is an amount deducted from their pay each week or month which will spend some years invested in the capital markets, but will eventually rematerialise as a pension. A minority have also interacted with the capital markets through receiving free shares, either as part of a privatisation of a former government enterprise or as a consequence of a conversion of a building society into a bank. In this instance, the enterprise or society has made a present of a future cash payment stream (the future dividends), which some members of the public have chosen to sell in exchange for immediate cash.

A still smaller minority are involved with the capital markets as owners of various securities. The conservative government of 1979-1997 tried very hard to get people interested in investing in the capital markets, and they succeeded in increasing the shareholding population from about two million to about eight. This group, still only 14% of the population, was courted by a range of companies who were anxious to sell personal equity plans, insurance savings plans, investment trust programmes, tax exempt special savings accounts, and an array of other offerings. The labour government of 1997 seems inclined to continue to support this form of saving. Clearly a four-fold increase in the number of shareholders is quite a substantial change, but it would be fair to say that the British people did not really grab at the opportunity to become shareholders. They seem to prefer to have someone else do this task for them. Unit trusts and pension funds fulfil this role.

In the United States, a very large number of people have decided to put their savings to work through the capital markets, especially through the mutual fund industry. Personal pension saving is very common, and the enthusiasm with which Americans have adopted this idea has pushed the principal stock market index over ten thousand, massively up from its level of one thousand in the early 1980s.

The extensive interactions which most members of the public have with the relatively mundane retail segments of the capital markets has done little to help the majority to understand what the capital markets' more significant, or perhaps just more esoteric, participants are actually up to. We know what a building society teller does, more or less. But what does a bond trader do? What is an option, and in what circumstances is it a good thing to buy or to sell? What is a swap loan? What does a fund manager do, and why do the newspapers report that they are very highly paid? What is a derivative? If someone says I have a greasy future, should I laugh, cry, or hit him?

Every profession develops its own shorthand and its own internally efficient language. Medieval theologians protected their thoughts from the masses by putting them all into Latin. The doctors know how to quell rebellious patients by talking of "benign cancers", which must sound like the ultimate oxymoron to the uninitiated. The finance profession probably created their own shorthand for the same reason as did the older professions, economy of verbiage. The consequent difficulty which those who are not close to the financial markets have with the terminology is regarded, by at least some insiders, as an advantage. Moles and Terry have recently published a very thorough dictionary, which gives clear explanations of the meanings of thousands of terms. We will only consider a tiny fraction of them in this chapter, or indeed in this book.

It is important to remember the conventional Saturday market. The sophisticated products of the capital markets lend themselves to circumlocution, but these products are always means through which something can be bought or sold. There are really only five different kinds of activity which the capital markets make possible. There are hundreds of variants, but only five basic kinds.

[1]   The first task of the entities comprising the capital markets is one of collecting money from people (or organisations) who have too much of it for their current needs, under contracts which are likely to permit the owners to get it back and which will reward the owners sufficiently to induce them to part with it. The simplest example of this is the acceptance of a deposit by a building society.

[2]   Secondly, the market entities are providing money to people and organisations who have a current need of more money than they have, under contracts which are likely to require the recipients to reimburse later and which will put the recipients under an obligation to reward, or

attempt to reward, the entity and thence the depositor. An advance to a business to buy a machine would be an instance.

[3]   Thirdly the entities act, on behalf of clients, to change the clients' level of exposure to risk. If we think, for instance, that dollars are going to get more expensive before we go on a trip to the USA, we might be inclined to go to an exchange bureau and buy them now, to eliminate our exposure to the risk of a later exchange rate change. On a corporate scale, the commoner action to achieve the same effect would be to buy an option. An option to buy dollars in a few months time at a price that is known now would leave us free to buy the dollars in the market if the price did not rise, but would limit the cost to a known extent if the price did rise. Obviously, an American confronting the opposite uncertainty might decide to purchase an option in Euros.

[4]   A fourth category of action would be to invest a balance in a contract in the hope of subsequent resale of that contract for a larger amount. Buying a share in another company would be an example. Some market entities act as brokers in arranging such purchases (or sales), others "make the market", acting as shopkeepers who will buy or sell on their own account.

[5]   The fifth category of transaction involves shifting a commitment through time. For a farmer, the ability to sell his September crop in March may give him a very valuable level of certainty. The concept of a future contract deals with this element of the work of the capital markets.

In every instance, the workers in the capital markets are trying to fulfil the goals of the boards of the companies they are working for. These companies are nearly all financial institutions, whose directors have the same objectives as those of other private sector companies for the most part. They want the firm to continue to exist. They would like it to become more prominent within its industry or within its country. They would like to obtain the esteem of their shareholders by providing a dividend, preferably a slightly higher one that they were able to provide last year. Above all, the directors would very much like to ensure that there are no nasty surprises; it is very bad for one's image as a director if you have to tell the world that something very bad has happened, and that you did not know it was going to happen. It is, in fact, not only bad for one's image, but also for one's career as a director.

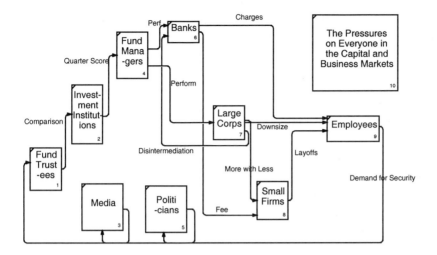

Diagram Two:- Pressures are exerted on everyone who works in the capital markets by other operators. The circle of pressure is complete, nobody is free from it.

Diagram two shows the forces which are being exerted on the institutions which will be discussed in this chapter. The diagram also conceptually illustrates the circular nature of the pressures. As each entity feels pressure on itself, it exerts pressure on the next. This pressure is transmitted round the entire loop and re-enters the picture at the left hand side again. The reader may feel that the pressure, named "demand for security" in the diagram, exerted by employees on pension fund trustees and other investment houses is rather weaker than many of the others illustrated, but it must be remembered that the employees are not on their own in this matter. The newspapers are very active in their support, the government is conscious of the need for security felt by the voters/employees, and the regulators, such as the Securities and Investment Board in the UK or the Securities and Exchange Commission in the USA and the various stock exchanges are in varying degrees vigilant on their behalf.

The Institutions:- [a] the Banks

From about 1940 until about 1970 it was an easy task to be a director of a financial institution. In Britain, banks would lend large amounts to major corporate clients at, say, 9%, having borrowed the funds in the capital markets or from the public for, perhaps, 6.5%. This colossal spread of 2.5% provided for a very generous level of expenses and remuneration to all the people who worked for the bank, and especially those at the top. It was relatively easy for the employees to make sure there were no nasty surprises.

The collecting and providing tasks were fairly straightforward, and usually involved assisting clients to time-shift one or more of their commitments, either by investment or by a future contract. The exposure risk was confined to the possible bankruptcy of a major borrower, and the security investment task was more or less ignored, the funds being provided to clients directly instead. The occasional major bankruptcy of a client was even helpful, in that it provided a rationale for the 2.5% spread; unpleasant for the client, unpleasant for the particular banker who had lent to that client, but pretty helpful to everyone else. "Those were the days, my friend, we thought they'd never end....." as the pop ballad of the 1960's put it.

From about 1970, however, the good old days for the commercial bankers came to a gradual end. The cause was simple enough. The major industrial sector companies worked out that they were at least as credit worthy as the major commercial banks, and if the bankers could borrow at 6.5%, then so could the industrial firms. And so it proved. The major industrial borrowers went directly to the market, and the banks were left with the second tier and smaller companies to lend to. This process was called disintermediation, as the bank ceased to be a necessary intermediary between the major corporations and the capital markets. This very considerable pressure is shown in the diagram as being exerted by the large corporations on the banking sector. Bank lending dropped steadily and the banks were forced to cut back on every kind of expenditure. They started a search for alternative sources of income. In due course, they found that the two best such sources were fee-earning services and consolidation.

The concept of a fee earning service was not new. In the older days, the high level of interest spread had allowed the banks to provide many services without specific charge for them. Under the new regime, the banks began to charge fees. At first, it was a matter of charging a fee for a formerly free service, which made the banks very unpopular indeed. They were able to muscle their way through that difficulty. Later, it became apparent that the total fees obtained thus were not going to be enough to sustain the shareholders of the banks (nor the senior managers either, for that matter) in the manner to which they had become accustomed. Banks and other institutions started to seek out opportunities to provide fee-generating services which were completely new. These fees and charges are shown in the diagram as forces exerted by the banks on smaller companies and on individual employees. They were much less able to exert pressures on the large corporations. Many new banking products have been invented, however, which are of considerable interest to the large corporations, and which bring together the bank's need for additional revenue with the clients' need for a number of jobs to be done.

One of the main classes of new products is the class known as derivative securities. These are contracts which have no intrinsic value, but which derive their value from their linkage with another contract which does have an intrinsic value. A share, for example, has an intrinsic value, being a specific fraction of the value of an entire corporation. An option to buy a share is a valuable right, but that value is derived from the value of the original share. We will take a close look at options later.

A second large group of new products are swap loans. A company which is seeking money in a market where the company is not well known would find the ordinary sources of finance rather expensive. A British company seeking finance for the first time in Brazil might be in this situation, for instance. A Brazilian company which was needing pounds would be in the same difficulty, only the other way round. Both companies would save themselves a considerable amount if each could borrow in its home country, where it is known and where it can borrow at a relatively cheap rate, and then swap the two cash sums. That is exactly what a currency loan swap involves.

These and other innovations have grown greatly in volume in the last twenty years. 42% of all the companies in America now (1995) use derivatives (FT, July 7 1997) and 30% of British companies have used them at some time (1993 or earlier)(FT May 1994). The chairman of Citibank UK was reported as saying that more loans were raised in 1992 by multinational companies for the purpose of swapping them than were raised for direct use. We will look further at these and some other innovations later on in this chapter.

Besides product innovation, the second solution bankers adopted to their revenue shortfall problem was consolidation. In the USA there have been two hundred bank mergers since 1990, with associated staff reductions. In the UK there have been few mergers, because there are very few banks to start with, but each of the banks has cut its staffing levels severely. One of the largest has cut its staff by a third to 26000. These reductions in headcount have been accompanied by substantial senior management emphasis on cost-effectiveness, so that the surviving bank staff are likely to be more aware than before of the possible conflicts between bank income and customer service. Previously, bank staff had been taught to think of customer service as a means of creating bank income. Now, the services which staff can make available to clients are constrained by quite detailed instructions on the limits to service.

The Institutions:- [b] the Corporations

It has been pointed out above that the big companies decided that they would not pay the high spreads of the post-war period. This did not happen all at once, but was a steady process of realisation, amongst the corporate bosses, that they did not really need the bankers except for a specific and limited range of jobs. For big companies, well capable of handling all their own multi-currency assets and liabilities, the list of jobs they needed the bankers for was very short.

The major corporations were not exempt from external pressures, however. In the same way that they were leaning hard on the banks for a better deal, the capital markets, usually in the form of big institutional shareholders, were leaning on them. Between 1960 and 1985, the proportion of the shares of the companies quoted on the London Exchange which was held by the institutional shareholders moved from about a quarter to about two-thirds. It is now quite common for a major company to find that human shareholders own only a tenth or a fifth or its shares. There is (I have been advised by an insider) one company in the hundred share index (the biggest corporations of all) which does not have any human shareholders at all. All its shareholders are pension funds, insurance companies, investment trusts, and similar entities. Most of these, of course, are run by humans, though some of the passive funds are effectively managed by a computer.

The institutional shareholders were a fairly docile lot in the 1960's. They would awake from their torpor if a takeover bid was proposed, or if a major corporation seemed likely to go under, but most of the time they let the managers get on with the task. Most managers, to their credit, did exactly that, but there were a few companies which were managed very sleepily indeed. Over the last dozen years or so, the institutional shareholders have changed their approach. They are now raising lots of questions at annual meetings, and interrogating company chairman and managing directors about what they are planning to do next. Expectations of growth in earnings per share have been raised, and the managers of the corporate entity had better come up with a good story, and then follow that with an actual result that is pretty similar to the story. In diagram two, this was depicted as the pressure to perform, and the same kind of pressure was exerted by the institutional shareholders on the banks.

It was not too difficult for the directors of the corporations to come up with the first few improvements in earnings. There was quite a bit of fat in the system in the 1950's and there was still some fat in the early 1970's. By 1980, the fat was pretty well gone. The deep worldwide recession of 1981 had the effect of cleaning out most of the rubbish among the corporate entities. The institutional investors did not relax the pressure for improved results, however.

The directors of the corporations had to develop more and more new money-making ideas. Some of these were new products, occasionally a completely new industry. Others were economy measures designed to achieve the same results as before at lower cost. Every employee that could be done without was laid off. Every activity that could be done by employees who lived in a low wage country was moved to that country, and the expensive employees in the home country were laid off, some of them for life. Information technology was developed to enable a single person to do work that had required three or more previously.

Old factories, shops, and offices which had been in operation for substantial periods of time were examined with a new and fiercer scrutiny. In general, it was found that there were economies of scale to be had by closing them down. This was not because they were defective, in many instances, rather that there were genuine economies of scale obtainable by putting all the production into a single large unit, and, as a general rule, the newer facilities were the larger ones. The communities which depended on the old facility were not, as a matter of routine, given much in the way of assistance by the corporation, because that would have had the effect of eliminating part of the cost saving which the corporate officers had been struggling so hard to find.

The end product of all this was that the corporations gradually changed their role. From being rather brutal slave-driving task-masters in the later Victorian years, through a period of being paternalistic pillars of the civic communities between the wars, the corporations have now moved to a global role, willing to flit from continent to continent in search of a cheaper way to make the standardised product. They have to. The institutional shareholders will, they firmly believe, sell the company from under them if the board of directors do not come up with a continuing progression in performance.

In diagram two, these forces are shown as being exerted by the large corporations:- the arrow named "disintermediation" is the pressure they exert on the banks by refusing the borrow except at the finest terms; The arrow named "downsizing" is the pressure they exert on employees collectively and individually as they search for cost reductions; and the arrow named "more with less" is the pressure they exert on small sub-contracting companies to achieve further cost reductions.

It is important to note that the shareholders do not, necessarily, penalise long term thinking on the part of company managers. Companies that spend a lot on research and development do not get discounted by the market and/or sold off. The entities making up the market are quite ready to support a long product gestation period if they are told about them. A firm that claims to be investing for three years to get a profit in the fourth and thereafter, but announces a slippage to year five or six, will be greeted with some disappointment but with acceptance. If they announce another slippage in year six, the market will probably become exasperated and enforce change. It is not the long term thinking they dislike, nor is it the slippage. It is the second slippage, and the evidence it provides that the managers do not know what they are doing.

The Institutions:- [c] The Institutional Shareholders

The concept of a corporate pension fund is relatively new. There were a few in operation before the first world war, for the benefit of the directors and the most senior management employees. By the time world war two began, there were several hundred in operation which covered the same exalted group, and a handful that stretched down to the middle managers. It was not until the 1940s that the idea of a pension fund that would service the whole workforce was even thought of, and it took quite a while to get under way. Once started, however, they became a very powerful force. It does not take long for a fund which is receiving 4% or thereabouts of the wage bill of a company to accumulate enough capital to buy the company. For instance, suppose the company had a wage bill of 20% of revenues, and a profit margin of 5% of revenues, and a price-earnings ratio of a dozen, all of which numbers are quite easily attained. If the pension fund earned at the same rate as the company, the fund would reach a value equal to that of the company in 32 years. This assumes that few of the employees would reach pensionable age during that period, which is quite common for a new business with a young workforce. A pension fund which began in 1960 should have equalled the company in value by 1992. In practice, of course, the pension funds tended to do much better than equal the companies to which they were loosely affiliated, so the interval would be less. It is almost impossible for a pension fund to make a loss, while an industrial company can achieve this all too easily. A pension fund which is managed reasonably astuteiy can expect to have a "really good year" at least as often as the company to which it is affiliated. It is also fair to mention that most pension funds receive considerably more than 4% of the wage bill.

In addition to pension funds there are many other institutional investors, including investment trusts, unit trusts, and insurance funds. Each of these funds is created with a specific investment objective and orientation, but the impact of compound interest affects all of them. In the USA, the same thing is happening. The total value of all the mutual funds in the USA is well over five trillion dollars, $5,000,000,000,000, and the other funds are also large. These institutional investors are managed by groups of trustees, who may be elected by the unit-holders in the case of a mutual fund or a unit trust, or may be elected by the company in the case of a pension fund. As the size of the institutions grows, the trustees have become increasingly unwilling to carry out the investment management job themselves, and have therefore appointed specialised management companies to do the buying of shares, the selling, and the other tasks of maintaining the relationship with the originators of the fund.

Most of the fund management companies operate on the basis of a fee which is a percentage of the funds under management. If the fund is small, in the twenty million pound range, the normal fee of 2% will pay the fund management company £400,000. A fund of this size can be managed by a single part-time fund manager and a clerk. A bigger fund, with assets of a hundred million, might pay a fee of 1.2% or £1,200,000, and might require the services of three or four people. These values will only be sustainable if the fund manager produces reasonable results. It is perhaps not surprising that the fund management business is quite competitive.

There are several rating agencies, one of which is the WM Company which is based in Scotland, who make it their business to provide assessments of the performance of the fund management companies. This information is usually provided on a quarterly basis, so that the trustees of a pension fund can see whether their fund has done well or poorly relative to the others over the most recent period. If it has done reasonably well, the trustees will tend to re-appoint the fund management company without much debate. If it has done badly, the trustees will probably take no action after the first poor quarter. After two poor quarters they will be asking quite fierce questions. Three poor quarters and they will be looking for a new fund manager. It follows that the fund managers are rather anxious to make sure that the companies in which they invest are generating financially successful results.

In diagram two, these pressures are depicted by the arrow marked "comparison", under which the trustees use WM data or similar to work out whether the investment institution they currently use should be retained or replaced, and the arrow marked "Quarter Score" under which the investment institution scrutinises the work of the fund manager.

The pressure exerted by the trustees on the fund managers is therefore transmitted to the managers of the companies in which the fund managers have invested the pension fund money. It is important to note that while a fund manager can make significant changes to the portfolio of shares he invests in during a quarter, it is very unlikely that the manager of an industrial company can make any major changes to his business during such a short period of time. The pressures exerted by the fund manager, acting on behalf of the pension fund, is therefore a source of considerable irritation to the manager of the industrial firm, because there is very little he can do to deal with the problem in the short term. An industrial manager may be able to take action to change his firm's performance over a three or four year horizon, but he cannot do anything in a quarter. As was pointed out above, most fund managers know this, and are willing to accept delay in the achievement if it is well signalled. There are a few fund managers, however, who do not seem to have grasped this point, and their antics have infected the whole relationship between industrial managers and the institutional investment communities.

For these reasons, many industrial managers have developed the practice of keeping some profit gains which they think they can achieve in reserve. Instead of putting these cost savings or revenue earners into immediate operation, the manager may choose to hold them back. In this way, the profits of the industrial firm may be caused to grow at a steady pace, using the discretionary profit increases to fill up any gaps which might suddenly appear in the profit pattern. The bankers and the fund managers do not like surprises, and the industrial managers may be able to satisfy their needs by keeping some ideas in reserve, for use when there is the corporate equivalent of a "rainy day".

Other Pressures:- [d] Technology

The growth in pressures which have arisen from institutional causes has now been sketched, perhaps sufficiently. These are not the only sources of pressure, however. There are at least two other sources of pressure, namely new product ideas and new technology.

When one looks back to 1960, it is easy to recall that the transmission of information was different then. There were letters, telephones, telex, and telegrams. Now, there are letters, telephones, facsimile, electronic mail, swiftair, internet, and voicemail. The time it takes to get a written message to a different part of the planet has reduced somewhat, but the cost of sending it has fallen dramatically.

When one looks back to 1960, it is similarly easy to note that the information available about companies was materially different from what is available now. There was a reasonable amount of data about the companies in one's own country, though it was usually at least six months to a year out of date. Those who were prepared to pay a substantial premium could also obtain data about the most important companies in the USA, Britain, Canada, or France. The data would be in the form of a printed set of accounts, and this might be accompanied by a review from a stockbroker who was following that company or that group.

Now, there are dozens of computer based data sources, capable of giving the subscriber any financial fact desired about the company at the push of a button, and capable also of dealing with any company that is quoted in any organised stock market on the planet. Analysts comments can be obtained in summary over the internet, and in more exact detail to subscribers over the fax machine. News of this kind has made it possible to create unit trusts and mutual funds of global reach. The total invested in these international, global, and emerging market funds has grown to

$370 billions in April 1997. There were 183 of these funds in New York alone at the same date. There was no possibility of having such an entity at all in 1960, much less of having 183 of them:- the information was simply not available with adequate speed or accuracy.

The speed and facility of data transmission is technically spectacular. Many of us have tried out the Internet, either on our own machines or at one of the very popular Cybercafes, where we can engage in a dialogue with someone on the opposite side of the planet, and can search for, and expect to find, other people who have special interests similar to our own. A business school in Cyprus, at which I have taught from time to time, used the Internet to find a specialist business librarian who speaks and reads Greek and has a degree in business librarianship including database management. She was in Saskatchewan, Canada, and would never have seen one of their normal advertisements. We can consult databases about any subject under the sun, using one of the "browser" programmes designed for this task. I would assert, but cannot prove, that the databases available in the financial field are by a substantial margin the most numerous, the most detailed, and the most widely deployed. Some are private, owned by individuals or by institutions, but there are dozens of major databases which are offered for subscription, and dozens more which are provided without charge as "advertising" by various consultancy and other service firms.

The availability of data about companies and markets in other countries is truly spectacular. It is also, perhaps, a little bit frightening and a little bit misleading. Databases are specially designed computer files into which you can place any kind of information you think you will be able to use. The main attribute of a database is that you can rearrange the data, so that the instances you are most interested in come together. For instance, you can sort a database of companies to bring out the ones whose sales have grown most rapidly, or the ones which have the highest price to earnings ratio. Databases are less good at dealing with qualitative matters. It would be possible to include data concerning a company's contributions to the cities in which it operates, but I have never seen that feature. It would be possible to include data about the number of fully trained apprentices the company has produced in a year, but I have not seen that in any financial data base either. Instead, the data are all financial results. Contributions to the city, and spending on training would not (usually) be shown separately, but would affect the database only by reducing the amount of the reported profit. If a company wants to make itself attractive to the international shareholders, the board would be well advised to take action to increase those numbers which show up in the database, and not spend money and effort on things which may produce long term benefit but which produce no database impact now.

When international investing is growing, and it was certainly growing quickly in the first half of 1998, it is almost inevitable that greater emphasis will be put on those features which can be obtained easily over the internet or from data bases. Many international investors employ local custodians and local sub-managers to help them to do their investing, but unfortunately this does not guarantee that the qualitative and local issues will be properly considered. The international investor uses the database numbers to evaluate the performance of the sub-manager, so the local knowledge of the latter is not likely to come to the fore. The sub-manager wants to keep the contract, and is therefore likely to concentrate on the database items his bosses are going to examine, and to give only moderate emphasis to the qualitative and the longer term aspects.

Much of what is happening in international investment is good for the investee countries as well as for the investor. Jobs are created, wealth is created, and wealth is transferred to places it was not previously to be found. The data base technology has been a major factor in making this possible. The technology tends to focus very sharply on the few key profit indicators, however. The civilisation, the communities, the culture, and other features of the investee site are not considered. These features are not the object of deliberate attack by the investors or by the technology, of course. But sometimes you need to give purposeful thought to a subject (such as a community) as a deliberate action which is part of the investment procedure, in order to avoid attacking it by accident.

Other Pressures:- [e] Product Innovations

It has been suggested earlier that the banks and the institutional investors and the corporations have been working harder and harder as the last fifty years have passed. The big corporations found they did not really need the banks, the institutions found they could squeeze more out of the corporations, and the fund managers acting for the institutions were frightened into putting pressure on all the private sector firms, including the banks as well as the corporate entities. It looked like a downward spiral. Each group of entities was trying to compensate for the revenues they had lost by levying higher prices on the others. This was a kind of vicious circle, and there simply was not enough resource available to satisfy the demands in aggregate.

One major element in the search for a solution to this impasse was that the banks, the corporations, and the institutions consulted each other intensely to try to find ways they could be mutually helpful. The need for a better profit record was the common goal, the question was whether they could help each other in ways that would improve all their results. The answer, or at least an important part of the answer, was innovation.

In 1960, the funding of corporations was a relatively simple matter. The company would issue ordinary shares (common stock in the USA) and might also issue preference shares. If it wanted some additional and more flexible capital, it would arrange a bank overdraft (British) or a bank loan (USA). There were a few other options available, but they were so expensive that they were seldom employed.

When the pressures came in the 1970s and the 1980s, the banks consulted with the corporations to find out exactly what they needed in terms of financial contracts, and devised a range of new products. The concept of an option had been known for many years, but it was not until 1971 that the Black Scholes paper came out which showed how these instruments should be valued. Before that, nobody knew how to price an option, and they were very hard to sell. From that date forward, the option became a vital part of the finance directors' toolboxes.

A call option is a contract that gives its owner the right to buy a particular asset at a future date, at a price which is decided as a part of the contract. A put option gives its owner the right to sell. It might, for instance, be possible to buy for a pound the right to buy a specific share five months from now for five pounds. The share price now might be, say, four pounds. If I was firmly committed to deliver this share to another person in six months, I could, of course, simply buy the share now and sit and wait.; That would cost me four pounds. Alternatively, I could buy the option for a pound. If the share price fell, I could forget the option and simply buy the share cheaply in the market. If the price rose rapidly, to ten pounds, say, I could simply exercise my option and obtain my share for five pounds plus the pound for the option, a total of six. By using the option, I have limited the cost of obtaining the share to a maximum of six pounds, for an initial outlay of only one pound.

This protection can be very valuable in guarding against serious fluctuations in the market price of various tradable assets. An insurer, for instance, faced with a large obligation after the imminent death of a rich client, might buy a put option governing the assets he expects to sell to pay off the policy. This will protect him from a sudden drop in their value. After the death, the insurer knows he will be able to dispose of the assets, because he has bought the right to do so. The insurer does not need to be so cautious as he would have had to be before options were readily available. Previously, the insurer would have had to dispose of the assets earlier, perhaps missing out on a last minute price surge, because he was too frightened of the possible loss when the sale gets closer.

We have shown how an option can be a good way to buy protection. It can also be a cheap way to buy risk. If you believe some share is going to move in price by a lot, the way to maximise your profit for a given investment is (probably) to buy a call option if the price is going to go up or a put option if the price is going to go down. This action is very risky, however, and the arrival of this product innovation imposes serious ethical question on those who sell the options. We may well have no qualms about selling an option to Citigroup, which can look after itself; but should we sell one to the Church Commissioners, who merely think they can?

Another derivative is a futures contract. There have been futures contracts for centuries. Nearly all the early ones were arranged by farmers who wanted to sell their crop at a known figure before the growing season began. These farmers were quite willing to accept a modest price in exchange for the assurance that they would not be faced with the ruination of a glut. More recently, it has become possible to enter into futures contracts for most of the world's currencies, for most commodities, for sheep fleece (washed and unwashed), and for a hundred other standardised products for which the manufacturer, farmer, or miner is willing to take a low price in exchange for certainty. A futures contract for unwashed sheep fleece is a "greasy future" so your reaction to being told you had one might be anywhere from delight to despondency, but would probably not entail assault.

It would be possible to go into a discussion of many more derivative products and many other financing products, such as swaps, which have arrived on the scene in the last twenty years, but there is little point. The present mission is not to address the nature of the product innovations which have occurred, but the consequences of their arrival. It would be sufficient to say, perhaps, that more than half the items on any list of financing products have been invented since 1980. That, of course, is not the same as saying half the financial transactions are using the new inventions. Some of these innovations have ethical consequences, and not all of these have yet been properly thought through yet.

Other Influences:- [f] The Delegation of Pressure

In section [e] above we have identified some of the more positive consequences of the pressures which have been felt by the large enterprises. Faced with serious declines in their traditional sources of revenue, the big banks and the big corporations have tried to innovate and to introduce new services which help the other big enterprises solve their revenue deficiency problem while also contributing to the profits of the innovator. The big institutional investors have also, to a considerable degree, pitched in; they have helped to finance some of the innovative small firms which are acting as the implementation vehicles for these new services. They have also supported the big banks and the big corporations as they seek to introduce the innovations.

There has been a negative side. The drop in real revenues of the big banks from the major corporations has been very great. The product and service innovations have been a big help, but they have not been enough to fill the gap. Similarly, the big corporations are having to work harder and harder to satisfy the institutional shareholders thirst for growth. One of the ways the big banks and companies have dealt with the problem is to delegate the pressure.

A fashionable word in the management literature over the last twenty years has been "outsourcing". Another is "downsizing". Two fashionable phrases have been "sticking to your knitting", and "core business". It is worth while to spend a few seconds on what each of these means. Outsourcing means getting a task done by a sub-contracting company which used to be done by employees of your own organisation. This usually has the effect of requiring the main company to have periodic negotiations with the outsource as to the nature of the task to be done and the scale of fees to be paid. It is possible, in these situations, for the main company to exert some pressure on the outsource to "do more with less". This means fulfilling the same or a larger task roster with the same or a smaller real cost. It is perfectly true that there is no reason why the same search for operational efficiency could not take place when the jobs are done internally; it is a simple fact, though, that the search either does not happen, or happens in a rather lackadaisical fashion, because everyone knows that the contract will not be lost. With an outsource, that assurance is not present.

The two phrases, "sticking to your knitting" and "core business", can be dealt with together. The first of these was put forward by Peters and Waterman in their now somewhat discredited book "In Search of Excellence", and is almost the only part of that book's list of ideas which is still generally valued. It advises the managers of a major firm to remember what they are good at, and to recall that the company they are running is achieving good results because it has built up a body of expertise in one or a few fields. Dissipation of their efforts into other areas, however superficially attractive they may appear, is dangerous and liable to cause serious distress if not failure. The concept of a core business is slightly different, but related. It requires the senior managers of the company to recognise that the market for their areas of expertise is not static, and that the expertise they must sustain is not an expertise in a particular science but an expertise in solving a particular class of industrial problems. The managers must ensure that the core business, in that sense of an industrial problem class, is focussed upon with the intensity of a laser beam. If a managerial group does that, the personnel of the company very rapidly divide into two groups. There are those whose work is central to the core business of the company, and there those who add to the cost base but who, regardless of their industry and efficiency, are never going to improve the core business. It is a fairly simple matter to move on to the next step, which is to outsource the non-critical.

All of this discussion may sound very sensible and very focussed, but it has a number of awkward corollaries and consequences. In the first place, if a company is going to outsource, there must be someone to whom it can delegate the task. You cannot just dump the task overboard and expect that the external world will pick it up and run with it, in a seamless transition from the internal execution of the same task. Secondly, the delegation of a task to an external entity automatically means that the external entity has some rights over the way the task is done. They may find it easier to serve their portfolio of clients by using a different method from that which the main company is accustomed to.

Thirdly, and most relevant to our main topic in this book, there is no paternalistic relationship between the parties. The downsized and outsourced task will, we must assume, be handled on a basis of good professional standards, paid for in full by the fee, but with no common feeling involved. If the performers of this task have any feeling of pride in their work, it will be pride in service of Little Ltd, not pride in the service provided to Big Ltd. By delegating out the pressure, Big Ltd has also delegated out one of the more valuable devices for handling that pressure, esprit de corps. In this area, British and American businesses have been absorbing the concept of company families from the Japanese. The major Japanese firms achieve much of their astonishing growth and progress from two causes. First, they have enjoyed extremely, perhaps dangerously, cheap capital until recently. Secondly, and more importantly for our present purposes, they have been able to farm out their uncertainties to the smaller firms that supply them with components. These smaller firms in turn farm out the uncertainties to yet smaller firms, and so on down the line. In due course, we reach tiny, one or two man firms, who may move from working twenty hours a day in March to working twenty hours in the whole of April, and who risk losing their status as a supplier if they ever were so daring as to take a holiday. This is not an aspect of Japanese business which receives a lot of attention, but perhaps it ought to. In diagram two, the pressure related to outsourcing and to other forms of subcontracting is indicated by an arrow called "more with less". Certainly, a lot can be achieved by making this demand, but there must eventually be a limit to its productive potential. In the Japanese case, it is possible that the severe financial difficulties which were observed during the summer of 1998 were caused, or at least worsened, by the combination of the continued action of the "more with less" force and the concurrent upward pressure on capital cost.

(g) Summary of the Problem Domain

The above sketch of the problem domain is, inevitably, a generalisation from a considerable array of observations. It will, therefore, be possible to find counter-instances to many, perhaps to all, of the pressures and influences which this chapter has considered. There has, nonetheless, been palpable change in the financial environment over the last thirty years. The easy ride of the 1950s will never return.

The principal force that has been at work in the field of finance in the last thirty years has been the concept of "shareholder value". There is a very major push in progress toward the promotion and enhancement of shareholder value. This phrase is hard to object to on its own. The shareholders have put in the money to get the venture into operation, and they are surely entitled to have their interests looked after by the management team which they, the shareholders, have put in place for that precise purpose. The literature of finance and the economists who write in the newspapers are unanimously in favour of the idea. The shareholders' long-term welfare, they all agree, should be the cornerstone of corporate policy.

There was a period when an alternative was put forward, to the effect that the company ought to be managed to cope adequately with the welfare of the stakeholders. These people were variously defined, and certainly included the shareholders, but also included the employees, the customers, the suppliers, and various other groups who interacted with the company on a fairly serious scale. The stakeholder theorists held that these others had rights, and ought to be consulted and ought to have an influence on policy. This idea has more or less died away now, for a variety of reasons, of which the most influential is probably the straightforward fact that the stakeholders (other than the shareholders) do not have any rights at all in terms of formulating the policy of a company. Creditors and employees have a right to get paid an agreed amount. Customers have a right to obtain a product that works, and so on. It would be a rather dim bunch of shareholders who would instruct their managers to run the place without taking customers needs into consideration. However, these other stakeholders have no right to say how the company should conduct its business. For this reason, stakeholder theory has more or less died away.

It would be difficult now to find a major company that does not at least pay lip service to the concept of shareholder value, and most of them are trying hard to put the concept to work in reality. This means they will close down a factory if they cannot sell the product it has been making for a high enough price. If an employee is fifty and no longer up to the job, the shareholders will get more value if we make him redundant than if we carry him as a passenger for ten years. If we can make a product in Kinshasa for seventy pence a unit, as against a hundred and forty in Cambuslang, then shareholder value will be enhanced if we move the production to Africa forthwith.

The search for shareholder value is a part of the mission of all the entities which have been discussed in this chapter. In some of them, it is the whole of that mission. The corporation and the banks obviously have shareholders, most of them institutions. Many of the investment institutions also have shareholders or very close equivalents, as is the case for investment trusts, mutual funds, unit trusts, and insurance companies, and the search for shareholder value is present in these also. Even the pension funds, and other investment institutions which have no shareholders, are also seeking to maximise "pensioner value" or whatever the equivalent is.

It will be part of the argument of later chapters that the ethical financier must think through the impact of his actions on an array of communities, of which the shareholder are only one example, and arrive at a balance in his decisions. Move production to Kinshasa, perhaps, but first (or concurrently) take steps to look after the communities affected in Cambuslang. Shareholder value will not be maximised if we so alienate the communities we operate in that a global vengeance campaign begins, which is already happening to a few companies.

Nestle, for instance, is still the subject of a series of negative campaigns, at least some of which can be traced to the controversy surrounding its distribution of artificial baby milk in third world countries. It seems likely that the senior management of Nestle would choose to handle that situation in a different manner from the one they chose at the time, if a second chance were to be available.

The task of the present chapter was in five parts. [1] To list a number of the more significant entities which are active in the capital markets, and which collectively comprise these markets. [2] To discuss what these entities do, and how their activities have changed over the last twenty years or so. [3] To show that there has been an increase in the pressure to perform, where performance is measured almost exclusively in terms of present and future financial results. [4] To discuss how the entities have tried to deal with the pressure to perform, namely by innovation in all aspects of their work, by combining their efforts with those of other similar entities, by ever-more-strenuous efforts at being economical and cost-efficient, and by attempting to farm out the pressures to other companies or other communities. [5] In these discussions, it has been suggested that the recent heavy emphasis on managing to enhance "shareholder value" is a very powerful influence already, and is growing both more powerful and more widespread geographically.

This chapter is not concerned with ethics, but is intended to set the scene for a discussion of some ethical questions later.

Chapter Two:- A Focus on the Problem We Are Addressing

In this short chapter, we shall examine two important writings, and also try to define exactly what the moral problem we are wanting to address looks like. The problem obviously grows out of the heavy and growing pressures on capital market people which were discussed in chapter one, but at this juncture it looks rather too diffuse, and perhaps also rather too large, to be manageable at all. The two writings are Steven Kerr's important paper "On the Folly of Rewarding A while Hoping for B", and a book by Milton Friedman. He has written many on the topic of "Capitalism and Freedom", but we will be looking at the one which bears that exact title.

The title of Kerr's paper is a rather good summary of it. He points out that there is no point in expecting the personnel of any organisation to ignore the reward system that exists in that organisation. If you want the employees to do something, then you ought to make sure that the reward system supports that desire. Unfortunately, there are many counter examples. He gives details, in the form of case histories in eight enterprises, where the reward system motivates the staff to do things the proprietors definitely do not want. We shall look at a selection; his point is obvious, but this is vital to our understanding of the capital markets.

Kerr's Case 1. In universities, the senior officials want the teachers to be very good at teaching so that the students will be well-educated and enthusiastic ambassadors for the university. The staff are only promoted, however, if they spend every minute they can squeeze out of the teaching grind to produce more and more published research. This paper was written in 1975, and the situation does not seem to have changed much.

Kerr's Case 2. In an insurance company, the medical insurance department kept careful records of complaints and returned cheques, so as to monitor and reward accuracy in claim payment. Few clients complained about over-payments. The clerks, therefore, could achieve a good score on the monitoring system by paying out too much. If a clerk was in any doubt about whether a claim should be reimbursed for a low cost or a high cost procedure, he would pay out for the high one. This potentially disastrous systemic defect was alleviated by the smallness of the difference it made to their pay. The employees received a 5% pay increase if they scored highly on the monitoring system and a 4% increase if they were "adequate", so most of them were pretty well indifferent about how many errors they made.

The clerks in this insurer were also subject to a rule that they forfeited the increase if they were absent from work three times or more in any six month period. This severe penalty could be avoided, of course, by stretching out the second illness until six months and one day after the first illness had ended. When a young worker had been off for two months in a year, his salary stopped and he received only sick pay at 30%. However, a worker with ten years service or more would receive sick pay at 90% of normal. The company, in effect, was hoping for good performance, but was actually rewarding attendance. What it got, therefore, was attendance.

Kerr's Case 3. In a survey at a manufacturing company, the senior managers were concerned that the middle and lower managers were not being adventurous or proactive. A survey showed that there was a very widespread belief, supported by extensive anecdotal histories, that the way you got approval from the high officers was to [1] set easy goals and attain them, [2] refrain from setting any demanding goals, [3] always agree with what your superior said, however daft, [4] always go along with the majority, [5] stay on the good side of everyone, and [6] always delegate risky decisions upwards. In such an atmosphere, it is a wonder anything got done at all.

In the context of the financial industry, which Kerr did not address, the point he is making is especially apposite. The reward systems are designed to reward activity. A bond trader gets a fee for selling a bond, he gets a fee for buying a bond. The department gets a portion of the profit that may arise when a bond they buy goes up in value, and the trader will probably get a bonus which is partly based on that profit. The bonus is an important component of his remuneration, but it is not as important as the activity fees for buying and selling. An equity trader is usually compensated on a rather similar basis. A commercial bank is nowadays always on the lookout for an activity which it can persuade a client company to engage in, for which it can then charge a fee. Interest, though still a major source of income for commercial banks, is much less significant than it used to be. In each instance, the emphasis is on activity. Do something, and you will get paid. If you do nothing, you will not normally be rewarded.

The income of a fund management company is a percentage of the funds under management. This might seem like a reward for inaction, and so it is in the very short term. If a fund manager chooses to leave the client's portfolio absolutely untouched, and it performs reasonably or better, the manager will indeed be rewarded for his inaction. This is relatively unusual though. Managers usually have to make quite a number of adjustments to a portfolio during a quarter-year to stay in the upper quartile by performance.

The people who work in the capital markets are, generally, rewarded for buying things that then go up in price and for selling things that then go down in price. The actions for which they are rewarded are "economic activities", in the sense of a purchase or a sale. The reward is likely to be a function of the profit contribution generated by these actions. He will share in the gains either as a direct percentage or (more probably) through some kind of bonus computation.

He is not rewarded for being explicitly ethical. He is not rewarded for being explicitly unethical. Any time he spends on giving attention to ethical or moral considerations and issues which are implicit in his work is simply subtracted from the time he can spend on buying and selling.

The capital market company he works for is quite likely to have a mission statement which solemnly intones the mantras of business ethicality. It also has, almost certainly, a substantial rule book saying when he can make trades and when he cannot, and setting forth a list of "thou shalt nots" to avoid transgressing the Financial Services Act of 1986 (UK) or the Investment Companies Act of 1940 as amended (USA). Specific rewards for ethical behaviour are just not provided. Spending time on taking specifically ethical actions will entail the loss of an opportunity to earn rewards. It is surely unrealistic to hope for ethical behaviour when we reward only profit and the avoidance of crime.

We have learned an idea of value from Kerr. Now it is necessary to do battle with Friedman. He has made a very large number of sensible points in his time, but there is one that must be fought with vigour. In "Capitalism and Freedom", and in several other books, Friedman argues that:-

"Few trends could so thoroughly undermine the very foundations of our free society as the acceptance by corporate officials of a social responsibility other than to make as much money for the stockholders as possible. This is a fundamentally subversive doctrine. If businessmen do have a social responsibility other than making maximum profits for stockholders, how are they to know what it is? Can self-selected private individuals decide what the social interest is? Can they decide how great a burden they are justified in placing on themselves or their stockholders to serve that social interest? Is it tolerable that these public functions of taxation, expenditure, and control be exercised by people who happen at the moment to be in charge of particular enterprises, chosen for those posts by strictly private groups? If business men are civil servants rather than the employees of their stockholders then in a democracy they will, sooner or later, be chosen by the public techniques of election and appointment" [Friedman, 1962, 133]

In a free economy, Friedman argues, the sole responsibility of business is to use its resources and engage in activities designed to increase its profits, as long as it does so through free and open competition, without deception or fraud. Friedman argues this case from the viewpoint of a liberal, by which he means a European liberal of the nineteenth century kind, who was not in favour of any avoidable intrusion upon the freedom of all citizens to do what they liked as long as they did no harm to the remainder.

It must be made clear that Friedman is not saying that nothing should be done, for instance, to assist the poorer members of society. In the same book, he specifically covers this point.

"It can be argued that private charity is insufficient because benefits from it accrue to people other than those who make the gifts....... I am distressed by the sight of poverty; I benefit when it is alleviated; but my benefit is the same whether I pay for its alleviation or someone else does. .... Suppose one accepts, as I do, this line of reasoning as justifying governmental action to alleviate poverty: to set, as it were, a floor under the standard of life of every person in the community. In that event we confront the problem of how to do it. .... In the first place, a programme should be designed to help a poor farmer because he is poor, not because he is a farmer. Programmes should never be designed to help occupational groups, or age groups, or wage-rate groups, or labour organisations, or industries. The programmes should be aimed to help the poor. Secondly, the programme should, while working through the market, not distort that market or impede its functioning. This is a defect of price support systems, minimum-wage laws, and the like" [Friedman, 1962, 191]

There is a considerable amount of support for this viewpoint from other economists, from students of politics, politicians, and others. Friedman is saying that the government has a duty to "put a floor under the standard of living" of everyone. His plea is that they should refrain from causing damage in the process. Let each functionary fulfil his function, and in particular let the businessman get on with being a businessman, and do not try to convert him into being a part-time welfare agency as well. He will, Friedman suggests, be rather seriously bad at it.

Normally, the present author would be very much in favour of these two lines of argument. Businessmen, in my own limited experience, are not at their best when they try to behave like a charitable foundation. They are very good at setting them up, but their record at running them is (with a number of honourable exceptions) awful. The forcefulness and dominance which made them good at running a company means they do not really listen to the true needs of the people they are trying, with the best will in the world, to assist. Perhaps they cannot listen.

When the time comes to consider a financing of a corporate project, however, I find Friedman's ideas extremely dangerous. The idea that the business decisions can be taken at the outset, and that the government, the welfare agencies, and others will come along behind and "plug in the ethics at the end" is simply not workable and is very harmful. The buildup to a major corporate decision may take months or even years. Analyses, consultant's reports, surveys, construction plans, site visits, and other preparations will ensure that the economic and physical aspects of the decision are fully considered. It is quite ridiculous to anticipate that another agency can come along later, after the project has begun or perhaps even after it is completed, to add ethicality to the situation. Ethical aspects must be considered early.

It is absolutely essential that the ethical issues be built into the project planning process at a reasonably early stage, certainly before the decision is arrived at. It is a principal argument of this book that the financial institutions which are involved in a project should ensure that the ethical questions are taken into consideration as a part of the preparations for making the decision and for agreeing the financial structure and the financial package. Ethics cannot be tacked on at the end. Ethical considerations should be made to lie at the heart of the business action and the financing action, with just as prominent a role as legality, profitability, technical feasibility, and corporate strategic suitability.

The moral task of converting the world's financiers to the adoption of a totally ethical stance on all investment and divestment projects is too big.

It is also too diverse; there are many different ways of being unethical. The mission of the present project is to try to formulate the ethical message for financiers by distilling it from the writings of the originators or early apostles of four of the world's great religions. The attempt will then be made to take this distillation, and to try to deploy it in an effective way in the routine decision processes of business financing. For this to happen, it will be necessary to ensure that ethics are considered early, and that the reward systems in use in the finance houses promote such consideration, or at the very least do nothing to inhibit it. The distillation will be the task of the next part of the book, and the deployment will be the task of the concluding part.

Part Two:- Guidance from the Religions

Chapter Three:- Plan and Introduction to the Religious Guidance Chapters

In this part, which contains seven chapters including this very short one, the source documents of four religions will be examined to see what they have to tell us that should guide financial work morally. This part contains a very short encapsulation of what the four ethical projects say concerning business conduct, almost certainly in an oversimplified format. In addition to the original writings of the religion, contributions by either one or two historically important interpreters have also been consulted. These interpreters include Maimonides for Judaism, Calvin for Christianity, Al-Ghazzali for Islam, and Rajavaramuni for Buddhism.

Before starting this, it is necessary to answer two other questions. Why did I confine myself to religious sources? And why did I pick these four religions, given that there are dozens?

On the first question, it must be said at the outset that there is no intention to exclude non-religious sources from consideration as a permanent matter of policy. There are not many books available on financial ethics (as distinct from business ethics, which subject is well covered in the literature), and there is certainly room for quite a few more on this narrower topic. We have to start somewhere. I hope to write another piece on the guidance we would get on these topics from the ancient philosophers of China, for example, but that is for another day.

A second reason for the decision to stay with religious sources is that these sources have penetrated very deeply into the soul of humanity. Even the atheists who are most scornful of religions, and who attack them daily, are propounding alternatives which say the same things. More importantly, the capital market operatives who are the "target population" of this research are people. They have family histories. It is very probable that the family history will include inputs from one of the great religions, even if the individual is no longer an active adherent. It makes sense to build on the big religions, because that way there is a better chance that the ideas put forward will "strike a chord" with the moral memory of the members of the group who must be persuaded.

On the second question, concerning why I chose the four religions I did choose, a partial answer has already been given. They were chosen on two criteria, one of which was market share. There are two billion Christians and about one and half billion Moslems. The next in size is Hinduism at about three quarters of a billion, followed by Buddhism at a third of a billion. On a market share basis, Judaism is nowhere.

I have to record a failure on Hinduism. I read several books about that religion, which is the oldest of all religions [Bowes 1977, Hopkins 1924, Hume 1931]. I simply did not find any evidence of ethical guidance relevant to the business world at all. Hinduism is obviously a fascinating and intricate theology, but I was not able to locate its views on business, or, alternatively I did not understand them. I asked a number of experts on general theological matters, but this did not prove fruitful either. It seemed safer to omit Hinduism, and consider the next one down in market share size, which is Buddhism. If you, the reader, are a Hindu, then please, firstly, accept my apologies, and secondly, please write a book on Hindu financial ethics. I promise to buy a copy.

The second selection criterion was market share within the financial community. On the basis of personal interviews with some Japanese students who had been working in the Tokyo markets before starting their MBA studies, the decision to include Buddhism was confirmed on the basis of market share within the financial community. The students believed that there was a small number of adherents of Shinto working in the Tokyo capital markets, but that the great majority were Buddhists. A significant number of them, I was warned by one student, were to be regarded as "inert Buddhists".

The number of Jewish people working in the capital markets is vastly disproportionate to their total numbers. There are about fifteen million Jews altogether, but their involvement in the capital markets is almost certainly second, after Christianity and ahead of Buddhism. There are powerful historical reasons for this. For centuries, Jews were prohibited from almost every trade except that of lending money. As nearly everyone else was prohibited from lending money, it is not surprising that the Jewish people developed a significant comparative advantage in the field of finance, and this advantage is still present. One of the reasons for this continuing advantage is the role of law in finance. It would be possible to conduct a major study of the similarity between the financial laws managed in the USA by the Securities and Exchange Commission, and the rules of behaviour set forth in the various basic texts of Judaism. On the basis of my own very incomplete comparison, I believe there to be a considerable similarity, not only of the actual texts but also of the "ways of thinking". I do not mean that the SEC regulations favour Jewish people, not in the least. But the way they are written calls for the same kind of extreme detail of analysis and argumentation. It is not in the least surprising that Jewish children who are attending schools which teach the Jewish religious law grow up to be effective and resilient in an environment governed by SEC and similar regulations.

The remainder of this part of the book is a discussion of each of the four religions in turn, followed by a chapter which seeks common ground among them, and concludes with a chapter which translates these religious commands into edicts which a modern financial person could understand and adopt.

Within each of the four religion chapters, the material is gathered into five segments. These deal respectively with the way in which the religion deals with (1) justice and restitution, (2) charitable actions, (3) lending and interest and usury, (4) wealth and general management, and (5) the procedures within the religion for changing its own rules.

From time to time within the four religion chapters, the reader will note references which are additional to the normal attributions to the authorities in the bibliography. These additional references are of the form [*13], where the number will vary. The purpose of these references is explained in more detail in chapter eight, where the views of the religions are consolidated, and where the extent to which they agree with one another is assessed. The additional references are inserted in the text to identify the point at which each of the following list of subjects arises during the discussion of each religion. The religious source books tend to say the same things, but sometimes in rather different ways.

Each of the sourcebooks of each of the religions makes a statement, or several statements, instructing believers that they should obey the following orders.

1   Provide for the poor
2   Do not hoard essentials, especially food
3   Use fair scales, weights, and measures
4   Pay fair wages that do not oppress
5   Never divert funds from a juvenile trust
6   It is quite all right to be rich as long as you are not obsessed
7   Business, as a partner or principal, is an acceptable activity
8   Do not swear a false oath and testimony
9   Support the clergy
10   Sustain the community in which you live and work

In addition to these imperatives, the religious sources require the believers to pay attention to various instructions which have been laid out about the following topics.

11   Usury. The religions all discuss this, but very differently.
12   Bankruptcy. There is some diversity of opinion among the religions on how to handle this, though much less than for usury.
13   The duty to render aid. The religions are not in agreement with respect to how far this duty extends. Some emphasise the duty to close family only, others proclaim a universal duty.

Chapter Four:- The Jewish Tradition

The Mishneh Torah of Maimonides is a truly awe-inspiring work. That one single man, acting as physician to Saladin, as head of the Jewish community of his city, as a major contributor to the medical literature of the day, and without the advantage (or would it have been such?) of a rabbinical training, could produce such a massive and masterly work, is almost beyond belief. It is a compilation and commentary: it contains a statement of every important instruction in the Hebrew Bible, and adds every important rabbinical responsa commenting on each separate topic, up to the date of the Code. The need for this compilation was apparently very great. Each rabbi, when approached to say whether a particular action was or was not in accordance with the law, would give an answer. Sometimes they agreed with other responsae, sometimes they did not. The status of conflicting responsae was unclear and confusing. It seems that the umpiring system for choosing among responsae was not working. Moses ben Maimon, who spotted the need and then proceeded to meet it, was certainly one of the most illustrious of a very strong group who were working together at Cordoba late in the twelfth century. Since that time, there have been three other compilations of the evolving pile of responsae, and at least one rabbi thinks it is going to be necessary for a new one in the near future. It is not surprising that the task has not been tried yet; the job is getting more formidable by the hour.

In the present thesis we are interested only in a very tiny segment of the Jewish literature, that which deals with the management of finance. Maimonides dealt with this in book thirteen of his Code, and especially in Treatise 1 on Hiring, Treatise 2 on Borrowing and Depositing, and in Treatise 3 on Creditor and Debtor. It would appear that a significant portion of judicial procedures we are now using to deal with financial questions was known and in use amongst the Jewish population, at least in Spain, by about 1170. A number of more modern writings have been consulted, but they do not seem to offer much in the way of significant changes to the fundamental conceptual basis of finance as it was articulated by the ancient rabbinical tradition through Maimonides' compilation. The modern rabbinical tradition, I have been advised, continues to build on the work already done, and rarely reverses a firmly anchored body of thought.

In addition to the three Treatises mentioned above, book 13 of the Code also deals with a number of other commercial transactions, and states what is allowed and what is not. Treatise 4 is about pleading, and the general management of courts and the justiciary. Treatise 5 is about inheritance, and the general problem of dividing up estates. It is interesting to note that the normal rule of primogeniture which figures in much of British law is differently applied in Hebrew law. The first-born, who may inherit the entire real property and a pro-rata share of the moveable property in Britain, inherits only a share of the estate in Hebrew law. The share he gets is the same as any two other siblings get.

The business of finance, however, is our main concern, and it is dealt with in Treatises 1, 2, and 3. The first two can be treated together, in that they deal in rather similar ways with two related classes of transaction. Both involve the obtaining of an object or a building or an animal or another chattel by one person from another, on a temporary basis, which transaction may be initiated by either of them. In treatise one, the supplier of the chattel is paid by the other party, while in treatise two he is not paid. Treatise one, therefore, is dealing with hiring, while treatise two is dealing with borrowing. A loan of a chattel without compensation may be a matter of the lender doing a favour to the borrower by supplying something he needs. Alternatively, it may be that the borrower is doing the lender the favour, in taking custody of the chattel for a period of time. This might arise if the lender is going on a journey and the borrower is looking after his cow. A loan of a chattel with compensation is a more conventional rental or hiring arrangement, and might be expected to occur more frequently if the lender and the borrower were not previously acquainted.

In either situation, however, whether paid for or not, there is ample room for something to go wrong, and Maimonides spends many pages listing the various problems that can arise, and what the decisions of the rabbinical courts have been in settling them. The borrowed horse can drop dead. The borrowed house can catch fire. The rented vehicle may turn out to be stolen.

Justice and Restitution

In the discussion in the two Treatises, Maimonides reports a significant number of cases and variations of cases, and the overall objective of the rabbinical legislators seems to have been one of restitution and justice. If you rent a horse to drive a waterwheel and it dies while doing that, you do not have to make restitution to the owner because the eventual death and replacement of his horse is an occupational hazard he ought to have built into his pricing structure. If you rent a horse to drive a waterwheel, and then ride it in a race pulling a heavy cart, and it dies, then you have to buy the owner another one. You have violated the agreement, by misusing the beast, so you pay up.

If you rent a vehicle and its owner and put the vehicle to use for any purpose, and the vehicle is wrecked, then you do not have to pay any more than the original rental. The owner, being present, is supposed to be able to avoid this accident, and therefore has to bear the cost, even if you were the party who was negligent. This is true even if the "presence" of the owner is of a rather tenuous form. A case was cited where the renter went to the place of business of the owner, and while making the arrangements for the rental of an animal, asked for a glass of water. The service of providing the glass of water at the same time as the animal apparently classed the transaction as the rental of an animal with the owner, and the subsquent death of the horse during the rental period was classed as its owner's loss. It is sometimes necessary to split rather fine hairs in making these judgements.

In every case, if the express terms of the contract are written down and signed by (or on behalf of) both the parties, and also by witnesses if the contract is for something important, then there is no need for a court judgement to be made. The contract will rule, if the contract is a fair one, and if its terms cover the eventuality which has arisen. The court judgements over the years have merely built up a list of decisions, which will be used to bind the parties if they have failed to define their own agreement.

There are frequent requirements in the judgements reported in the code that one or other of the parties making a claim on the other should swear an oath as part of his evidence. In some instances this had to be a Pentateuchal oath, in others an "informal" oath. The penalties for swearing a false oath were severe, and could amount to death in really serious situations. [*8]

In almost every instance, the case law reported in the Code in this general category gave constraining instructions, rather than positive commands. Once the courts had said something, the word would quickly get around that some specific action, taken in some specific set of circumstances, was not allowed, and the generality of people would refrain from doing it. In the case of the glass of water mentioned above, for example, it would be safe to assume that the majority of vehicle renters would keep their various activities clearly separated from that day forward. The rabbinical courts did not, as a general rule, give positive instructions on how to conduct business. Instead, they gave negative instructions, of the form:- "Action X, in circumstances Y, is the responsibility of party Z, who must pay party Q to restore the situation". There were, however, a number of specific and positive instructions, which were exceptions to the general constraining approach.

Charitable Actions

The requirements to lend and to give to the poor of Israel [*1] without compensation, but possibly with restitution, is an absolute and clear positive order from several of the Hebrew Bible books [Deut 15:8 and 9]. There is a second set of positive commands which instructs Jews who lend to non-Jews to charge interest [Deut 15:3] or equivalent compensation; we will consider this topic later under usury [*11].

There is a set of rather tough laws which explain what is to happen when a creditor comes to the debtor and demands repayment. While it is an offence for the creditor to exact repayment from a debtor whom he knows to be unable to pay [Ex 22:24], the rights of the creditor in other situations are well protected. The demand having been made, the debtor is required to bring his assets, down to the last needle, and he is then given back food for a month, clothes for a year, and a few handtools to earn a living with, a couch and a bed. The rest (if needed) goes to the creditor [*12]. However, if the debtor has no assets, he goes free. If the creditor thinks he has hidden some, the creditor is not allowed to go into the house of the debtor to check. Apparently this reasonable protection of the home of the debtor caused the entire lending system to seize up, and rules had to be revised, allowing the creditor to pronounce anathema against the debtor, which (amongst other consequences) could be used to retrieve assets held by third parties which were the debtor's property. In addition, the income of the debtor, over and above bare subsistence, had to be paid to the creditor month by month, until the debt, but no interest, was paid off.

For the genuine poor, however, there was a specific and clear requirement to be of help. As agriculture was a very important industry at the time of the Hebrew Bible, and still at the time of Maimonides, the specific indications of what to do to help the poor were generally rural in style. When a harvest was taken in, the owner was not permitted to harvest the whole field, but had to leave a corner of it to enable the poor of the community to come in and harvest that [*2]. When a field had been harvested, the owner was not allowed to glean it, that is, to go over it again to pick up the items he had missed the first time. These had to be left to feed the poor. The owner would gather the harvest into sheaves, typically. If he found he had left a sheaf in the field when the rest had been taken into the barn, the owner was not allowed to go back for it. That sheaf had to be left for the poor as well.

In addition to these instructions, there was a general command [Numbers 18:29] that the generosity of a Jew should be proportional to his own financial status. "Out of all your gifts" you should make a donation to the poor. This clearly places the obligation on an approximate par with present-day income tax, which is roughly proportional to income and certainly requires more from the rich than from the poor.

Lending

The instructions in Deuteronomy 23, at verses 19 and 20, set the Jewish nation on track to develop and to dominate the banking industry for more than a thousand years. In a number of important areas, they still do. There are fourteen million Jews in a world population of 5.8 billions, which comes to a quarter of one percent. In a rapid survey of the published accounting reports to collect the names of those participating in banking partnerships, (mostly merchant or investment bankers) in 1994, the proportion with Jewish sounding surnames was forty percent. I do not pretend that this statistic is accurate, but it would be very surprising if it was wrong by a factor of 160. The Jewish bankers have served the worlds financial requirements very effectively and for a long time.

The rule is very specific. You are not allowed to take interest if you lend to a brother, which is taken to mean a fellow Jew [*11]. You are, however, required to charge interest when lending to "the heathen", which is everyone else. This is not an option, but a requirement [Deut 23:21]

In the Christian community, with its emphasis on universal brotherhood, the same passage was taken to be a prohibition on any form of interest charging at all. The combination of these two sets of requirements meant that the only form of interest bearing debt finance that could happen was when a Jew lent to a "heathen" and when a "heathen" lent to a Jew. There is a specific prohibition in the Code, [Book 13, Treatise 3, Chapter

5, Paragraph 5] which prevents Jews from borrowing from Jews with interest by using a Christian intermediary. There are several intricate rules for dealing with the situation in which either the debtor or the creditor converted to Judaism after the loan had been put into effect.

It is clear that the situation has changed since the middle ages. John Calvin lamented the impossibility of a law prohibiting interest in his commentary on Deuteronomy. The creation of the limited liability company has made it possible for Jewish company to lend to Jewish company in a manner that Jew cannot lend to Jew. At the same time, the provision in the Code which prohibits the oppressive collection of a debt by a creditor is still in operation as far as the rabbinate are concerned.

It is much less clear what the situation might be when the "financial oppressor" is a corporation. The corporation is secular, in general, and is not subject to the Jewish law. The protection which the rabbinical law affords to the debtor who is in dire straits financially is not available in this situation. It would appear that the secular law is the only one that matters in this situation, and that is the conventional law on bankruptcy. It is for note that the normal British law on personal bankruptcy is very like the provision of the Code of Maimonides [book 13, Treatise 3, Chapter 1, Paragraph 4] which has already been discussed, in which all the debtor's assets can be gathered together, certain vital necessities returned to him, and the rest sold for the benefit of the creditors [*12].

It is also perhaps interesting to note that the Jewish tradition had reached the stage of devising this relatively civilised approach to financial disaster by 1150, whereas the civil law of Britain on the topic was still prescribing imprisonment for certain debtors (thereby ensuring their inability to repay) until the Act of 1869. Jeremy Bentham (1843) is rather sarcastic on this point.

Wealth and General Management

In addition to the specific rulings on restitution and on justice, and the requirement to behave charitably, and the requirement to charge interest when dealing with non-Jews, there are quite a number of miscellaneous instructions which are intended to give broad guidance on how to behave in matters financial.

In the first place, there is a clear statement that wealth, on its own, is not to be regarded as evil [*7], but as an aspect of life that one should be careful about. If you find yourself getting rich, do not take this too seriously. [Psalms 62:10][*6]. Do not "set your heart upon it". Be watchful of yourself, so that you are not greedy and envious [Ecclesiastes 5:10-12]

In your behaviour, you should pay fair wages [Jer 22:13][*4], you should give correct weights and measures to your customers [Proverbs 16:11][*3], and when you are a trustee for a minor or someone disabled, you must never divert the funds to your own use [Proverbs 22:16][Zechariah 7:10][*5]. In addition, you are not to engage in speculative hoarding of life-essential materials [*2].

Procedures for Changing the Rules

The Jewish rules have come about through a series of rabbinic questions and answers, and the ability to ask these questions and obtain these answers means that the corpus of Jewish law is in a state of continual adjustment. There is no doubt that this change is slow. At the same time, there is a provision for change built into the system. Once in a while, an intellectual giant like Maimonides comes along and codifies everything, but there are many other minor changes being made almost daily.

A fascinating insight into this process was provided by Jacob Katz, in his 1989 book on the Shabbes Goy, which he subtitled "A Study in Halakhic Flexibility". His goal was to examine the process through which the Jewish rabbinical law evolved, and he used the law about working on Saturday as a case. It became quite apparent that the Jewish law prohibiting work on the Jewish sabbath was causing serious stress to the Jewish part of the economic system, especially in retailing, in many parts of Europe. This became especially acute when a Rabbi decreed that you could not get round this problem by hiring Christians to do the work on that particular day, because one's servants are subject to the same law as the Jewish employer, even if they were not Jewish themselves. This is not the time to recite the whole tale, but Katz makes it clear that the rabbinic law has a procedure within itself which enabled it to give ground, in this case and in others, rather slowly, to meet the needs of the people. There are, of course, some points which would never be changed. At the same time the advantage of having only a part of the law on tablets of stone is usefully demonstrated in Katz' contribution.

Chapter Five:- The Christian Tradition

In considering the Christian approach to the management of money and wealth, the principal source has been the Bible. Both Testaments have extensive coverage of the topic, though the matter is not dealt with in the precise fashion which one finds in the Jewish regulations. At the same time, the general message is made quite clear. The Gospel message known as the Golden Rule is not limited in its application to matters of finance, of course, but it provides a solid starting point for financial as well as for other aspects of ethical thinking.
"Therefore all things whatsoever ye would that men should do to you, do ye even so to them: for this is the law and the prophets." [Mark 7:12, also Luke 6:31]

In addition to the Bible, we refer to a few of Calvin's commentaries, and to useful proceedings of occasional conferences on the interface between God and Mammon. These include Occasional Papers of the Centre for Theology and Public issues, especially number 11 on "Finance and Ethics" and number 23 on "Vision and Prophecy", as well as the excellent earlier conference on "Ethics in the World of Finance" edited by R Hopps.

Justice and Restitution

The Old Testament, which overlaps in large measure with the Hebrew Bible, is laden with ferocious promises about what will happen to readers who misbehave. Tribes might obstruct the path of the children of Israel militarily, "But the Lord thy God shall deliver them unto thee, and shall destroy them with a mighty destruction, until they be destroyed". [Deuteronomy 7:23]

Individual persons were subject to threats of at least the same ferocity, for a substantial list of offences. "And I will come near to you to judgment; and I will be a swift witness against the sorcerers, and against the adulterers, and against false swearers, and against those that oppress the hireling in his wages, the widow, and the fatherless, and that turn aside the stranger from his right, and fear not me, saith the Lord of hosts." [Malachi 3:5] Zechariah is similarly tough on people who oppress the poor. [Zechariah 7:10]

The writers of the Proverbs promise a rather milder fate, of penury, to those who oppress the poor, namely that "he that oppresseth the poor to increase his riches, and he that giveth to the rich, shall surely come to want." [Prov 22:16]   The Old Testament is also very hard on usury, which we will consider below in the segment on lending.   As a general rule, it may be argued that the Old Testament view on most kinds of offences is that the offender should put the plaintiff and the state back where they were before his offence happened. The stolen goods should be returned or replaced with better ones. A serious offender should be punished with a suitable heavy sentence. They seemed to be trying, long before W S Gilbert thought of the phrase, to make the punishment fit the crime.

There appears to be a considerable feeling at present that this is quite a sound approach. Lawmakers in many Christianish countries seem inclined to impose sentences of increasing length in the hope of stemming the rate of increase of crime. This is not the place to discuss the social science of penology. It may, however, be noted that the fierce penalties of the Old Testament were generally meted out in a context of a solid tribal society which, we may safely assume, exerted strong social pressure against the commission of crimes. It may be assumed quite reasonably that one would have to work quite hard at being an alienated outcast before you reached the stage of being punished. It is easier to reach that status now.

When we move to the New Testament, the approach changes drastically. Perhaps the most extreme example of this is in Paul's letter to Romans. "Recompense to no man evil for evil. Provide things honest in the sight of all men. If it be possible, as much as lieth in you, live peaceably with all men. Dearly beloved, avenge not yourselves, but rather give place unto wrath: for it is written, Vengeance is mine; I will repay, saith the Lord. Therefore if thine enemy hunger, feed him; if he thirst, give him drink: for in so doing thou shalt heap coals of fire on his head. Be not overcome of evil, but overcome evil with good." [Romans 12:17-21]

The emphasis is on the general concepts of love and of forgiving. The phrasing is still combative, however. By feeding your enemy, you improve your chances of obtaining a favourable result, compared, we must assume, to tackling him by armed combat.

The Christian message advocates much the same treatment for the poor, but for a different reason. The enmity of the enemy may be smothered by love, but the poor simply need help. The passage about the judgement scene, in which the "sheep"and "goats" are separated by the

King of Heaven, makes it clear that looking after other people who need help of various kinds is the sort of behaviour that Jesus wants from his troops. "And the King shall answer and say unto them, Verily I say unto you, inasmuch as ye have done it unto one of the least of these my brethren, ye have done it unto me." [Matthew 25:40]

This topic will be revisited under the heading of charitable actions below, but it is important to note that the Christian rules impose a severe penalty on those who ignore or fail to feed the poor [*1]. Justice, in other words, will be done. It may not happen in the current life, but it will surely happen in the life beyond.

The idea of a Christian community is also a strong force in the New Testament. The Christians are encouraged to be mutually supportive in everything they do, helping each other along the path towards the "perfection" that Jesus has set as the target. In a discussion of roles in a christian community, Birch and Rasmussen define a vision of the community morality in what they call a minimal form. "The environment must be open and tolerant. Persons very different from one another must be free to express themselves without recrimination. There must exist a basic respect for persons, all persons, as bearers of the image of God. All must be accorded a fundamental dignity as creatures of God, and heard as children of God". [Birch & Rasmussen, 1989, 109]. The community concept is even more forcibly argued by Rasmussen in his plea for a rejuvenation of the active church in the USA, entitled Moral Fragments and Moral Community [*10]. He complains that the society is coming to pieces, and that the church is one of the agencies which ought to repair it, and that the church will only do this if it leads in the task of moral formation. This involves adopting practices (catechisms, watchnight services, communion, etc) as a way of life. It involves making the church a haven during turmoil. And it involves taking a role as a moral critic, for reasons similar to those given by St Paul in Romans 12. [Rasmussen 1993]

A community is an alternative to having to administer justice by means of a court, and legalistic methods. It is a means also of trying to reduce the number of incidents which require restitution to be invoked. It certainly seeks to avoid the number of incidents entailing retribution. The community approach certainly does not prevent arguments, but it may make their resolution more gentle.

Not every New Testament writer is completely sold on the concept that retributive actions may be avoided. The fiery words of James may serve to remind us that quite a few Christians, then as now, were determined on revenge as punishment for current wrongs. "Go to now, ye rich men, weep and howl for your miseries that shall come upon you. Your riches are corrupted, and your garments are motheaten. Your gold and silver is cankered; and the rust of them shall be a witness against you, and shall eat your flesh as it were fire. Ye have heaped treasure together for the last days. Behold, the hire of the labourers who have reaped down your fields, which is fraudulently withheld by you, crieth: and the cries of them which have reaped are entered into the ears of the Lord of Sabaoth. Ye have lived in pleasure on the earth, and been wanton; ye have nourished your hearts, as in a day of slaughter. Ye have condemned and killed the just; and he doth not resist you." [James 5:1-6]

Charitable Actions

The original Christian teaching on charitable actions is a very close relative of the Jewish teaching which had grown up alongside it, though the Christian version appears to be considerably less precise in its formulation. The general command is given in Matthew 19:21, with the story of the wealthy youth who had kept all the commandments but was unwilling to obey the last instruction. "Go and sell what you have and give to the poor, and you will have treasure in heaven". The Jewish order to give to the poor is much more precise, stating how much you should give to the poor, and giving guidelines about the importance of looking after self and family as well.

The Christian text seems to require a general asset realisation. The words of Jesus quoted in Matthew 19:21 do not say that the wealthy youth should give it ALL to the poor, merely that he should give to the poor. However, the youth seems to have understood it to mean a total divestment, and refused to co-operate. This is not surprising. Christians have been doing much the same ever since.

At the same time, it is universally understood that the basic obligations of a Christian include the requirement to make charitable donations. In very large measure indeed, the Christians have done exactly that over the centuries. In this regard they seem to have been guided by St Luke, as he wrote in the Acts. "Then the disciples, every man according to his ability, determined to send relief unto the brethren which dwelt in Judaea" [Acts 11:29]

Notice that this text leaves the assessment of the amount to the donor, while making it clear that the rich should be the financial mainstays of the project. It is also for note that the relief was intended for "brethren". This was a response to the report of one Agabus, who had told them there was going to be a serious famine. The Christians of Antioch decided to have a whip round and send the proceeds to help their colleagues in Judaea, and Barnabas and Paul were assigned the job of taking the collection there. It can be presumed that there were other people situated in Judaea besides the Christians, and that these others would be similarly hurt by the famine. The Christians of Antioch nonetheless chose to make their donations to the Christians of Judaea, not to the populace at large [*13].

Much later, during the lifetime of Calvin, the obligation of wealthy Christians was re-examined by that eminent pastor. Innes gives a very detailed discussion of Calvin's views on financial and economic affairs, and prefaces the discussion with the remark that Calvin was the first theologian ever to take the trouble to understand how the economy did work before he made pronouncements about how it ought to work.

"(In Calvin's opinion) it was the duty of wealthy Christians to remember what Christ had taught and to provide for the less fortunate. No longer was it the prerogative of the pious rich to give to the needy at whim just to help earn their soul's salvation. Since man was justified by faith alone, self-seeking charity would not save the sinner. For Calvin, giving alms was to be expected, an obligation. Its only spiritual reward was to help the donor live in closer communion with God. .... more than simple charity was called for. Some redistribution of wealth through ready employment and fair wages was necessary. It was equally important to eliminate practices which threatened the well-being of the badly impoverished. Specifically, Calvin condemned speculation, hoarding, and profiteering on essential commodities, especially food." [Innes, 1983, 244][*2][*4]

Calvin was rigorous in the way he examined a financial activity. Before he made any pronouncement about it, he would check to see what the transaction in question did as a practical matter, and would judge it to see if it conformed to Christ's law of compassion.   In the second half of the quote above, we see that Calvin did not think that simple charity was going to be sufficient to get the standard of living of the poor up to a high enough level. Wage rates had to be at a sufficient level [*4]. Further, some of the special sins of the asset management industry were examined and listed for eradication, not because of the profit element, but because of the damage they could do to the poorer members of the society.

As a concluding item on this topic, it may also be said that the Christian writers over the years have emphasised the need for a "progressive taxation" regime in the charity field. The rich should give proportionately more generously than the poor. The story of the widow's mite, in which the poor gave proportionately more than the rich, is a salutation to the lady in question, not a recommended procedure for general adoption. The only Biblical reference that seems to deal with the topic is in the book of Numbers, and therefore of Jewish rather than Christian origin. It is not written to advocate progressive donation, only proportional donation. "Out of all your gifts ye shall offer every heave offering of the Lord, of all the best thereof, even the hallowed part thereof out of it." [Num 18:29] This reference is clearly written to require donations which are proportional to the assets of the donor. It is not so obvious that the rich should donate proportionately more than their poorer colleagues.

Lending

Interest on lent funds has been a controversial topic in the churches for a long time. At the Council of Arles in 314AD, clergymen of the Christian church were prohibited from taking interest on loans. This prohibition was repeated at the Council of Nicea, eleven years later. The rules got tighter and tighter, with laymen being prevented from taking interest in 348AD (Carthage), and again in 789AD (Aix), 1179 (Lateran Council 3), 1274 (Lyons Council 2). It must be presumed that the habit of taking interest on loans was breaking out again and again at regular intervals, otherwise there would not have been much point in repetitive prohibitions. Eventually, the Council of Vienna got so fed up with it that they decided in 1311 that anyone who engaged in usury was a heretic.

Fowler [1979,27] has observed that the only real effect of these numerous prohibitions was to strengthen the financial role of the Jews. Monarchs, who were as prone to deficit financing in the first millenium as they have proved to be during the second, simply evaded the prohibition, and the churches could do nothing about it. To get round the prohibition technically, the monarchs would invite the Jews into their country to lend the funds needed for assorted public sector projects. The Jews were further concentrated into the banking field by the additional constraint in some nations, that the monarchs would not permit them to engage in any other line of work.

The Jewish regulations on the topic have already been covered in chapter four. The general rule is that Jews cannot lend to other Jews on interest, but they can, and indeed have an obligation to, charge interest to all other borrowers. [Deuteronomy 23:19-20]

The hard line against interest in the Christian community seems to have held firm until about 1500. It was not that interest was not being paid on loans prior to that time, but simply that official notice had not been taken of it. There were many exceptions, and many verbal contortions to make the realities fit the image. There are quite a few situations in which one party wants to have the temporary use of some money belonging to someone else, and is quite happy to pay a fee to the other party for letting them have the use of it. This is, of course, interest. The fact that the church was against it was an inconvenience, nothing more, which tended to put the price up a bit. Certainly, there would be no point in anyone lending money to someone else without an interest payment, except in cases where the borrower was a close relative. The religious reformers and leaders in Switzerland, among whom Calvin was very prominent, tried very hard to stop the charging of interest within the city of Geneva and elsewhere, for the same Old Testament reasons as had been used for centuries. They failed; the people who wanted to borrow just invented clever dodges to circumvent the prohibition, and the Council of religious leaders could do nothing about it.

One of the devices used to get round the interest prohibition was the concept of a loyer. The hospitals of Geneva wanted an income to arise from the substantial endowments they were being given by rich patients and patrons. Since interest was not allowed, they took the asset which the patron had given them and rented it to a tenant, for a few years, during which period he had to pay the hospital a twentieth of its value, and after which he either had to return the asset to the hospital, or renew the rental. The hospital's asset could be money. In this situation, the difference between the "rent" which the tenant was paying and the payment of interest is purely semantic.

The practical need for interest continued unabated, as more and more projects were launched all over Geneva. About 1510 in Switzerland, the problem began to be serious. The Franciscans were trying to help the poor by lending them money, amongst other methods. After much trial and error and an array of different methods, they simply found that the operation was not viable unless they charged a fee for the loans. Everyone agreed that the work the Franciscans were doing was great, and everyone agreed that the poor were much better off as a result of their loans and other efforts. Why, therefore, was the fee they had to charge a sin?

After extensive debate, the Lateran Council of 1515 accepted a motion that the Franciscans had not been sinning when they charged a fee for their loans to the poor [*11].

This opened a chink in the anti-usurists' armour, and there were many who sought to widen the hole. Interest became rapidly commonplace, despite the objections of Calvin and the rest of the religious Council. Eventually, the burghers of Geneva appointed a committee in 1557 to examine the situation. This committee should be the subject of at least a PhD thesis sometime, as its decision has had quite remarkable consequences. The committee, set up to review the accusations of the pastors (including Calvin) that there was usury about, came to the conclusion that there was indeed usury about, and that there was no way it could be avoided. For the avoidance of "fraud, destruction, and ruination", the charging of interest, said the committee, ought to be allowed.

The road to the modern banking industry had been declared open. The financing of ventures through a mixture of participations and debt is now thought of as normal. If the committee had not decided the way it did, we would have been forced to continue to use participations as the only way of supporting a venture, and even with limited liability the rate of progress would have been considerably slower.

Obviously, if the 1557 committee had decided against interest, that would not have been the end of the matter for good. We can never know how long it might have taken for a successor committee to be appointed and decide for interest, nor can we ever know how many committees and how many centuries it might have taken. In any event, the committee did act to open up the banking option for the Genevans, and other cities were close on their heels. Perhaps we have now, in 1997, gone beyond the point at which the innovation of allowing interest was a help. There can be little doubt, though, that some at least of the material advantages created between 1557 and 1997 have improved the lives of most, or at least many, of the people.

In modern times, we find ourselves thinking through the problem of debt once again. I had the privilege of speaking to a conference on the topic in May 1996, when the head of the Anglican Church delegation to the United Nations arranged for a batch of bishops and a flock of financiers to debate the problem of serious debt among the poorest countries. The World Bank and the IMF were represented, and a lot of useful ideas were exchanged. The shareholding governments of these institutions agreed to write off two thirds of the debt for the forty poorest countries shortly after this. I do not think the conference was the cause of this write-off, but it can have done little harm in terms of focussing the minds of those responsible on a topic they might have been happy to allow to drift on. The problem is still not fixed, as some of the very poor countries cannot even pay the interest on the remaining third.

The problem these countries confront is exactly the same as the problem which was annoying the prophet Nehemiah. The Jewish nobility of the day were charging interest on agribusiness loans at a stable rate, but the farming community did not have a price-support cartel in place nor was there a government department charged with stabilisation. There was a serious famine, and the farmers could not pay the interest. They were forced to sell their daughters and sons into slavery to pay the interest, and some of them lost ownership of their farms. Nehemiah and some associates had been working on negotiations with the slaveowners to buy the Jewish slaves out, and he became understandably cross when he found out that his own bosses had forced the slavery sale in the first place. Nehemiah organised a protest rally, and the nobles were given a serious ticking off. Nehemiah chapter five. The nobles agreed to stop charging interest, and to refund the interest already charged.

The poorest countries in the present era do not have the option of selling their children into slavery. Instead, they simply default on the loan, which therefore compounds upon itself. This is a chapter on Christian views, but the Quranic complaint about usury "doubling and redoubling" seems quite applicable. At an interest rate of 17%, a borrower who failed to pay the interest on a thousand pound loan would be owing 2200 pounds in total after five years. And 5000 after ten, and twenty thousand after nineteen, and a million after forty-four.   At some point in that sequence of compounding, a borrower who is earning a stable income will lose control of his situation. It may be early or late, depending on the size of his stable income, but the grinding mathematics of compound interest and default will get him in the end, if he is not able to pay up.

Various suggestions have been made on how this might be dealt with. Kunibert Raffer [1990] has shown how the bankruptcy laws might be adapted so that a country could obtain the same kind of protection as a company already can. Jeremy Bentham [1843] pointed out the futility of imprisoning debtors, and mentioned bankrupt nations as an additional example.

At the present time, however, it is the case that the Christian view about lending is that lending on interest is a permissible activity, provided the rate of interest charged is a reasonable reflection of the risks involved.

Wealth and General Management

The suspicions voiced by the religions on the subject of wealth are quite like one another. The Christian suspicions, however, include a noisy minority who go beyond the norm.

The norm appears to be rather well summarised by John Wesley, the initiator of the Methodist church. The Rev R Hubert Luke summarised John Wesley's standard sermon number 49, entitled the Use of Money, in the following terms. "The layman must gain all he can, by legal means, without harming himself or others, defrauding the State, or selling dangerous products.   Then, he must save all he can, avoiding the gratification of foolish or wrong desires. Third, he must give all he can, recalling that the money really belongs to God, and he is just a steward. After all necessary spending on self, family, and dependants, the rest must be given away". [Luke 1979 83][*7]

There is obviously a bit of room for negotiation on the exact quantification of the word "necessary" in Luke's discussion of Wesley's instruction.   There is a presumption that the personal spending should not be ostentatious, whether that ostentation was achieved by flaunted wealth or well-advertised asceticism. There is at least an implicit permission that the Christian is allowed to make provision for dependants after his own death as well as during his life. The hoarding of large amounts of money over and above these requirements is seen as pointless and unChristian [*6].

The norm also seems to have included a substantial amount of investment spending. As Innes has observed:- "Profiteering and speculation might be forbidden (by Calvin) but certainly not the investment of money to open a factory which benefitted the community by producing jobs and a new source of income. .... The entrepreneur devoting his energy and resources to a moral enterprise was right to pray for its success, though not on the basis of his personal gain." [Innes 1983, 247]

There was also a considerable agreement on the activities which should not be allowed. Calvin, after thinking it through to the best of his considerable abilities, vetoed speculation, hoarding, and profiteering on essential commodities, especially food [*2]. The reasoning, in essence, was that these activities were damaging or potentially damaging to those community members least able to cope with it. It is certainly true that the kinds of speculation practiced in the 1550s would almost certainly have increased commodity prices, which is not true of commodity speculation now.

A similar concern for the poor has more recently been expressed by the Catholic church in America. "The fulfillment of the basic needs of the poor is the highest priority. Personal decisions, policies of private and public bodies, and power relationships must all be evaluated by their effects on those who lack the minimum necessities of nutrition, housing, education, and health care. This principle recognises that meeting fundamental human needs must come before the fulfillment of desires for luxury consumer goods, for profits not conducive to the common good, and for unnecessary military hardware." [National Conference of Catholic Bishops, 1986, P46, Para 90]

The task of helping the poor can be fulfilled in part by charitable actions, as discussed in the previous section, but charity is not a very good long term solution to poverty. The recipients eventually become addicted to the charitable receipts, and stop trying to escape from it. The donors lose patience with the apparently wilful idleness of the recipients and become less and less willing to donate. The tax and benefits systems of some countries permit the continuation of charity as a money-transmission process for a while, but do little to foster community spirit in the process.

In general therefore, it may be appropriate to summarise the Christian view of wealth in the words of the Psalmist. "Trust not in oppression, and become not vain in robbery: if riches increase, set not your heart upon them." [Psalms 62:10] And again in the text of Ecclesiastes. "The sleep of a labouring man is sweet, whether he eat little or much: but the abundance of the rich will keep him awake at nights" [Eccles 5:12] [*6]

When it comes to general management issues, the religions are also in substantial agreement. The need to pay a decent living wage has been a theme of Christian writing down the centuries, just as it has figured in the other Holy books. See Jeremiah 22:13 [*4]. Obviously, there has been considerable controversy concerning how much that amounts to in cash terms, but the principle is solid enough. Honest dealing, giving full measure, accurate scales and weights, are all also endorsed. See Second Corinthians 13:7, Proverbs 16:11, Philippians 2:3-4 [*3]. It would, indeed, be a rather odd religion which said the opposite.

At the same time, we must keep a watchful eye on all business dealings. The chances of managers getting away for long with anything downright crooked is quite small, but there is quite a bit of room round the edges of business for judgements to be made, and there is often more pressure to veer towards profitability and away from brotherly love than there is in the opposite sense. The need for watchfulness is nowhere better phrased than in Amos. He claims to have been a shepherd, but he must also have been a substantial commodity trader, judging by his knowledge of the available dodges.

"Hear this, you who trample the needy and do away with the poor of the land. You who say 'when will the New Moon be over so that we can sell grain, and the sabbath over so that we can sell wheat', skimping the measures, boosting the prices, and cheating with dishonest scales. Buying the poor with silver and the needy for a pair of sandals, and selling wheat with the tares bound into the centre..... .. The Lord has sworn by the pride of Jacob that every act is written down." Amos 8:4-6.

Procedures for Changing the Rules

The Christian church does not seem to have any procedures for changing the rules on any significant subject. Changes seem to take place only by the building up of a colossal pressure for change, followed by a traumatic fight. After that, a part of the church follows the first option, another part follows the second option, and the two pieces of the church continue in parallel. This has happened repetitively over the last five centuries, and little progress has been made in putting the various small pieces of the church back together. Attempts to reunite any two pieces of the church tends to result in the creation of either three or four pieces. These are the people in piece A who did not want to join the merger, the people in piece B who did not want to join the merger, and the people who did want to join the merger. In some instances, the merger does not happen, in which case we may, at least temporarily, have four churches where there were only two.

This difficulty in dealing with change is not attributable to lack of procedural machinery. The church has enough committees, one might have thought, to deal with any possible topic. There are hierarchies of committees, so that subjects can be moved up and down the hierarchy without decision for generations. There are committees at each level with defined responsibilities. Only a proportion of the problems of the real world conform to these definitions, which enables each committee to pass the other topics round the other committees at its own level, sometimes for several complete circuits.

There are, in general, procedures for effecting change which seem to have the actual effect of stopping it. I am conscious of the possibility that the other religions discussed in this part of the thesis may also have the same organisational thromboses, and that it is simply because I am closer to the Christian religion that I find the Christian version especially noticeable and annoying.

At the same time, I think there is a fair amount of evidence for the general point I am making. The reformation only resulted in a split in the church because Rome would not adapt. Luther, Calvin, and Zwingli, as far as I can read, did not intend to set out a new church, they meant to straighten out some of the kinks in the existing one.

More recently, the adaptability of the churches has been tested again and again, but has not shown huge improvement since Luther's time. Namesake Martin Luther King 's letter from Birmingham jail [King 1986] reflects bitterly on the conservatism of the Christian clergy and the Christian hierarchy on racial matters during the 1960s. A major new branch of theology, Liberation Theology, has arisen, especially in South America and in south-east Asia, dedicated to improving the lot of the poorest members of society in a fashion which seems very consistent with the Gospel instructions. Gutierrez, Ellacuria, Segundo, and the others did not really want to create a parallel church. They wanted the existing church to do something for the poor, which would have saved them from a great deal of effort and danger. Ellacuria was shot for trying to sort out the land ownership system in El Salvador. The established church seemed to be placing itself consistently on the side of the leading families, who were deemed by the liberation theologians to be the source of the trouble. Once again, the church had failed to adapt. [Schubeck, 1993]

On financial matters, the churches have been fairly slow at adaptation also. Given the resource base of the churches, as they stood in 1900 or thereabouts, positive management of the funds should have increased the resource and the capability to fulfil the church missions steadily over the century. If positive management was seen as too advanced, perhaps simple competence might have been tried. That too would have built the endowments of the churches to an extent which would at least have allowed them to continue the mission at the level of operation prevailing in 1900. Instead, the financial and investment management of most of the churches has been delegated to a series of committees consisting of well-meaning but totally incompetent people who have a much clearer idea of how they would like to spend the money than they have on how to manage it for the future welfare of the church and its mission. The bizarre behaviour of Archbishop Marckincus and the horrifying ineptitude of the Church of England Commissioners will serve as the most extreme, but unfortunately not the only, pieces of evidence.

Chapter Six:- The Islamic Tradition

The Jewish tradition has had more than three thousand years to evolve, the Christian tradition has had almost exactly two thousand, while the Islamic tradition is in its 14th century at the time of writing. This obviously means that the Islamic tradition could draw upon the Jewish and the Christian traditions when this was considered desirable, and they have done so. Indeed, the tradition records that Ishmael, the elder son of Abraham, was the originating person behind the religion which Mohammed brought into such sharp focus in the years the Christians call 600AD and following. The Quran is, of course, the Islamic Holy Book, but the importance of the other writings is acknowledged within it. In Sura Five, "The Table" [Quran 5:48], we find:- "Surely we sent down the Torah, in which there is guidance and light........... and we sent, following in (the rabbis') footsteps, Jesus the son of Mary, confirming the Torah before him, and We gave to him the Gospel, wherein there is guidance and light......"

I have used Arberry's translation of the Quran for the most part, but have also used that of Ali to confirm some of the interpretations. I have found the Concordance of Kassis [1983] extremely helpful in finding relevant sections of the Quran, and have also found the two works of Montgomery Watt [1962 and 1979] to be most revealing. Most of the references are to the Sunni approach, not the Shi'ite.

The religion of Islam is equipped, as befits a religion with nearly a billion and a half adherents, with many interpreters and many commentators. The original script of the Quran was handed down and then written down within twenty years or so of the death of the Prophet in 632AD.   After that, a substantial body of additional material was gathered in the "Tradition", the hadith, which provided an accumulating body of observations and comments made by the Prophet or by the Companions. There were duplications and conflicts among these hadiths, and it became clear before long to the ulama (the collective term for the priesthood of Islam) that some of these hadiths were not genuine. The huge task of editing the hadith corpus down to the genuine sayings was undertaken by Al-Shafi'i of Cairo. His edition of the hadith has been widely accepted, and continues to be an important source of guidance now.

However, the eclectic nature of the Islamic tradition is also widely acknowledged by the authorities. A prominent commentator, Ignaz Goldziher (1910, p40) thought the willingness of Islam to draw in other sources was one of its strengths. He said "Whatever Islam produced on its own or borrowed from the outside was dressed up as hadith. In such form alien, borrowed matter was assimilated until its origin was unrecognisable. Passages from the Old and New Testaments, rabbinic sayings, quotes from apocryphal gospels, and doctrines of Greek philosophers and maxims of Persian and Indian wisdom gained entrance into Islam disguised as utterances of the Prophet. Even the Lord's Prayer occurs in well-authenticated hadith form. This was the form in which intruders from afar became directly or indirectly naturalised in Islam." It inevitably follows that there should be a substantial amount of common ground between the instructions of Islam and its predecessors. As we shall see, however, these instructions, at least on business, were far from being identical.

Ruthven has suggested that one of the reasons why the business instructions are not even more similar than they are was the separation of the church from the state in the Christian way. He observes [Ruthven 1984 p179], "It is important to note that there never was a real separation of church and state in the Islamic world, the way there is and has been in the Christian. The development of industrial activity was never impeded for individuals in Islam, but the state never really allowed a proper "burgher" class to develop, who might have financed and developed that activity. An exception was where the religious law conflicted with the wishes of the ruler, in which case the ruler would go his own way and the ulama could do nothing." It is for note that the Islamic countries with the most substantial business orientation appear to be the ones with the most secular governments, whether republican or monarchic.

Legal Principles of Islamic Justice and Restitution

The Quran itself contains relatively little that is to do with commercial law, and what there is is mainly about inheritance laws and laws about protecting women and children. The hadith, on the other hand, is full of legal material. Major schools of thought developed, and three of these were in a state of nearly permanent disputation. The school of Hanbal became known as the strictest or most fundamentally Islamic, and it has gained ground recently with the growth of the very literalist Wahhabi movement. The school of Hanifa tended to emphasise the need for pragmatism in the religious affairs, and was ingenious in inventing ways of re-interpreting Quranic prohibitions. The school of Malik was very moralistic, and paid close attention to the intentions of an actor in determining whether his actions were permissible or not. The school of Al-Shafi'i was founded by the pupils of that great codifier. He established the procedure for verifying which hadiths were valid as statements by the Prophet or one of the Companions and which were not. His school was dedicated to continuing the work, in making sure that the codification of the hadith was perpetuated, and that the new interpretations that became necessary were still able to be comprehended within the context of the Quran and the Sunna of Mohammed.

In a limited programme of reading of the legal decisions in the hadith, extracted from the writings of Al-Ghazali, I did not find anything very surprising, with respect to matters of restitution and justice.

The regulations on borrowing and repaying, however, seemed to be rather similar to those found in the Code of Maimonides [Quasem 1975]. Al-Ghazali was writing a century before Maimonides, and was writing in Baghdad, while Maimonides spent some of his time in Cairo and some in Cordoba. We may infer that the ideas of Al-Ghazali influenced Maimonides, or that they were both writing down, independently, the "common knowledge" of the time, in terms of commercial judgements.

In Al-Ghazali, the requirements to make restitution if an object was borrowed and then damaged were clearly stated. If the object was of poor quality or very old, the borrower could make restitution by means of a small cash payment. If it was new, the borrower had to replace the object to the satisfaction of the lender or make a cash payment that was satisfactory to the court. If the borrower could not repay, the lender was entitled to complain to the court, who could make any of three decisions. The court could declare the borrower "bereft", in which case the lender was given credit for having made a charitable donation to the poor. The court could declare the borrower bankrupt, in which case his possessions could be gathered and sold off, sufficiently to repay the loan, but without selling his house or his toolkit. Thirdly, the court could declare him corrupt, in which case he was made bankrupt and flogged as well. This was used if he had been fraudulent, especially in terms of hiding assets.

Charitable Actions

The Quran is very firm about charitable actions. It is not a voluntary activity, but an essential aspect of Islam. Consider the following extract from the Sura 89, The Dawn. "You are not generous towards the orphan, and you do not urge one another to feed the poor, and you devour the inheritance of others with devouring greed, and you love wealth with boundless love. .... On the judgement day all these offences will be remembered, and you will cry 'I wish I had listened to the commandments' " [Quran 89:17][*6][*1][*5]

The injunction to look after the poor appears again and again in the Quran, and is reinforced in the hadith at great length. The Quran, in the longest Sura, The Cow, contrasts demonstrative religiosity with true piety, which depends on firm belief, and also adds that "True piety is .... to pay the alms, to give of one's substance to kinsmen, orphans, needy, the traveller, the beggar, and to ransom the slave......... and to fulfil any covenants that you have entered into......." [Quran 2:173]

The first element of charity is the zakat, which is compulsory, amounting to one fortieth of the income of the donor. It is highly desirable for a good Muslim to make an additional voluntary donation, called sadaqa. However, there is no merit in impoverishing yourself to do good works. A major study of the arabian manuscripts in the Gotha Library by Pertsch established a series of instructions designed to limit charitable donations. "You are to stay fit and feed yourself so you can do the work of God. You are to give alms if you are financially secure, not otherwise, and to kinfolk first. The law provides for a measure of renunciation, and there is no merit in going beyond that". [Goldziher 1910, P123][*13]

In the business world, the normal behaviours concerning fair weights and measures are expected [*3]. However, there is a further list of meritorious actions which a business man could take, which would be deemed especially meritorious. This list was reported by Al-Ghazali as being the positively worthy actions of the man of affairs. There are six of them. [1] Do not exceed the normal profit margin [2] Buy from the poor at more than market [3] Sell or lend to the poor at a discount [4] Repay loans ahead of term, and repay with a better object than the object borrowed. [5] Rescind a sale if the buyer requests it, and do not enforce the contract [6] Sell food to the poor on credit, and do not call it in unless they become rich. [Umaruddin 1962]

Al-Ghazali made it clear that this group of instructions was a highly desirable set of actions, which would be borne in mind by Allah at the day of judgement. These are in a different category from the compulsory, basic, requirements for honest dealing. In a related segment of the text,

Al-Ghazali observes that the most devout men of business will desire for others what he desires for himself, will work to promote justice and beneficence, and will instruct others on how to be morally good traders.

These wishes may sound rather like pious hopes in today's market environment. Surely, however, it is not so long ago that merchants were "instructing others on how to be morally good traders"? I can recall having received some such instruction myself from my first boss. That is a while back, but hardly prehistory.

As Al-Ghazali is the most important of the interpreters we are using in this segment, it would be perhaps appropriate to take two more quotations from his magnum opus, the Ihya. The first of these is related to the bodily need to build wealth, the second to the spiritual need to dispose of some of it. "Sufficient wealth is necessary to achieve that bodily health which is essential for knowledge and action, the two primary means of happiness." [Al-Ghazali D,III,246,200,203 in Quasem][*7]. And again, "The highest grade of generosity is giving away wealth despite the owner's having need of it. This is altruism." [Al-Ghazali D,III,223, commenting on the Quran 59:9][*10]

Lending

The Islamic ban on usury is almost certainly the single attribute of that religion of which financiers are aware. A large proportion of the wealthiest people on earth work in the banking industry, and their normal reaction to the Islamic ban on interest is to burst out laughing. They "know" that the concept of interest is central to the economic development of the world, and that they and their predecessors have made a substantial contribution to that development process, and that they could never have done it if interest had not been possible. So they are scornful when they learn of a religion which banishes interest.

The issues relating to interest are discussed more fully in chapter eight. At this stage we report, as a matter of record, on what the Islamic authorities appear to mean by the term usury, for which their word is "riba". It is not, perhaps, very suprising that the word is not singular in its meaning. The meanings which can be applied to the word include:- [1] interest, [2] excessive interest, [3] any reward which depends on the passage of time and on nothing else. It would appear that the objection that is being raised to interest is to do with the absence of linkage with the project for which the money has been provided.

For instance, if the supplier of money were to buy shares in the business, so that he had, say, a quarter of it, there would be no riba. If the business were a success, the supplier of money would do well, and if it flopped he would also (to that extent) flop. The Islamic system is totally supportive of this kind of business involvement [*7].

If, instead, the same supplier of money were to supply the same amount of money to the same business on terms which provided that the business or its owner would pay that amount back in twelve months time, then there would be no riba. An interest free loan, designated as a borrowing, is not and cannot be usurious.

If, thirdly, the same supplier of money were to supply the same amount of money to the same business on terms which provided that the business or its owner would pay back that same amount in twelve months time, and that they would also pay the supplier a small amount of interest, we have a situation about which the Islamic discussants are not in agreement [*11]. Some use the word usury to mean any interest at all, in which case this third version would be usury. Some use the word to mean an excessive amount of interest, in which case this third edition would not be usury. The exact borderline between interest, and excessive interest, is not at all clear. One commentator suggested that interest was excessive when it was above the market interest rate, which is a difficult argument to sustain if you are starting from the proposition that there should not be any market for debt.

The basic argument against interest seems to be that the lender has not been a part of the business venture. He has done nothing to deserve a reward, either in terms of labour, or in terms of know-how, or in terms of supplying materials or tools. He is not taking the economic gamble of launching the business, with all the risks that step carries. He is simply supplying money, on terms which are as free of risk as his lawyers can arrange, thereby transferring all the risk (or as much of it as possible) on to the shoulders of the entrepreneur.

In the Quran, one of the major problems is not only the usury but the way in which it "doubles and redoubles". The origins of this phrase seem also to be controversial. It may refer to compounding of interest, which is a relatively common system now. Alternatively, it may refer to a penalty system in lending which may have been prevalent at the date of the Koran. Compound interest is a reasonably well understood phenomenon now. £100 invested at 20% compound will double in four years, redouble in 7.5 years, re-redouble in 11.5, and re-re-redouble in 15 years, reaching approximately £1600 at that time. The original supplier of the capital does not have to take any action to bring this about, except the initial action of getting the compound interest contract signed. The religious objections to this are apparently related to the absence of effort, involvement, or merit required from the supplier of capital.

A second objection to compound interest is that the requirement to repay may occur at a time when the debtor is in some financial difficulties, and there is a Quranic prohibition on chasing someone for a debt when the lender knows he cannot repay it. The arithmetic of compounding, as has been shown in the example above, can result in quite large numbers being involved in rather short periods of time, and the obligation can therefore grow beyond the reasonable competence of the debtor quite quickly if it is not repaid at the original (presumably quite early) date.

The other principal theory about the nature of riba is that it was a penalty. The idea here was that the borrower would borrow, say, £100 for one year at no interest. However, there would be a penalty of doubling if it was not repaid on time. At the end of year one, the borrower, let us suppose, could not pay the £100, so the debt suddenly jumps to £200. If he could not pay £100 in year one, there is a fair chance he will not be able to pay £200 in year two, so that puts the debt up to £400. This can, of course, continue indefinitely, with the debtor bankrupted at the will of the creditor. Apparently, according to Goldziher, it was quite common for people who got into this sort of mess to sell themselves into slavery in exchange for complete absolution from the debt. It would seem, from simple examination of the arithmetic, that they were already in a state of slavery when the redoubling of the penalty took the total above their annual cash inflow.

Whichever of these explanations of riba may have been the right one, the concerns of Mohammed and the writers of the hadith are easily understood. They simply did not want their people to be subject to the enslaving consequences of interest. Further, they took the view that the lenders should have had a better understanding of the will of God, and should never have written the contract so that it could have these kinds of enslaving results.

The prohibition on usury continues to the present. The Saudi banking law requires that the banks invest in equity participations, so that the return to the bank is a prorata share in the profits of the business, and is nothing to do with the length of time the money is invested.

At earlier times, there were various schemes to circumvent the prohibition against usury. Double sale contracts were the commonest. These were also prohibited by the hadith, but are actually very hard to catch. The way these contracts would work would be as follows. I agree to sell you my umbrella for a thousand pounds on January 1 1998. You agree to sell me the same umbrella for twelve hundred on January 1 1999. These two agreements are arrived at on the same day, and really constitute one agreement, but, for the purposes of avoiding the usury law, they are treated as two. What has really happened is that you have lent me a thousand pounds for a year at 20%.

One interesting aspect of the Islamic law is that the same prohibitions on usury which affect individuals applies to Islamic companies. This is an important difference from the Jewish system. Interest is routinely charged among Jewish companies, though not among Jewish individuals who are taking their religion at its face value

Wealth and General Management

The idea of operating your business at a profit was totally acceptable in the early days of Islam and remains so now. There was nothing wrong, in the eyes of the Prophet, with becoming well off. The problems with wealth were not really to do with the wealth itself but the tendency of some men to become excessively focussed upon it. There is a passage in the Quran which draws attention to this potential difficulty. "Woe onto him who amasses wealth and counts it as a safeguard, thinking that his wealth will make him live forever" [Ruthven, 1984, 65][*6,7]

In the same vein, the prominent early Islamic theologian Maududi wrote that there was nothing wrong with private wealth and property, provided these were employed for "the service of virtue and public welfare". The evils of capitalism are caused by the moral shortcomings of the rich, who fail to recognize the needs of the poor people, not by any innate problems of capitalist concepts and methods on their own. [Ruthven, 1984, 329]

The Prophet was rather hard on people who "put on airs", as we might now phrase it. He did not appreciate it if people who had wealth came before him in wretched clothing:- if God made you prosper, you should show it by wearing something sensible and appropriate to your financial situation. Another fellow, riding in a group to a meeting with the Prophet, was admired greatly by his fellow pilgrims because he was forever at prayer. Mohammed was scornful. "If this fellow was praying all the time, who was looking after his horse?" "The rest of us took turns to groom the horse" "In that case, you are showing greater merit than he did". In a similar way, the Prophet was more impressed by action than by talk. "Allah has given a higher rank to those who fight for his cause, engaging their wealth and their lives, than to those who sit still" [Quran 4:95]. Mohammed appears to have taken people as they were. Naturally, many of those he met were conventional business people of the time, accustomed to trading, retailing, or agriculture. The instructions he issued to these plain folk were therefore fairly plain too.

The basic virtues of honesty, generosity, and courage preached by Islam were much the same as the virtues prized among the chieftains and other leaders of the Bedouin. Up until Mohammed's time, it had been considered sufficient for the lower orders to display loyalty and obedience to the leaders of their clan. They had no individual responsibility for understanding what a moral virtue was, much less for behaving according to one. From the Quran forwards, though, this set of virtues was required of everyone, not just from the aristocracy. The low-born were also to be held responsible for their behaviour.

For the businessmen, the instructions in the Quran were traditional messages, saying nothing particularly new, but saying things which cannot be said too often by people who are leaders and influential. "Use fair measures and true weights when trading goods" [Quran 17:37, 83:1, 6:153, 7:85][*3]. "Pay fair wages to your workers" [Ten suras][*4]. "When you are a trustee, do not fraudulently convert any of the assets, but keep the estate intact for the benefit of the child" [Quran 4:12][*5]

Although the Prophet seems to have taken a rather pragmatic view of wealth, some of the theologians who followed behind were rather more sceptical. The Quran was quite clear that wealth itself was perfectly acceptable, provided it is properly deployed and not hoarded for its own sake [Quran 104:2, 25:67, 27:29] Al-Ghazali, however, was very nervous about wealth. Superfluous wealth, said the famous scholar, can cause at least four different kinds of trouble. [a] It facilitates the commission of sins. [b] Excess wealth may cause the enjoyment of permissible pleasure, which gradually extends to the doubtful, and to acquiring wealth in wrong ways [c] The wealth imposes cares and stress on its owner, who spends time looking after his wealth instead of on remembrance of God. And [d], wealth is something which can remove a novice from the Path. [Al-Ghazali D,III,200,202-5 in Quasem] Although it is clear that the status of the Quran is far higher than the status of even such a distinguished scholar as Al-Ghazali, the concerns which he was expressing in the above extract from the Ihya were quite influential in the determination of court cases.

On a more mundane level, Al-Ghazali also produced a list of prohibited actions which will prove quite important to our future discussions. In the Ihya [D,II,69-83] he writes about very important issues for the capital markets, though he probably had never heard of the term. His concerns in this situation related to the problems of hoarding, forging, and market information.

Hoarding food with a view to selling it high later was not prohibited if the food in question is in good supply. However, it is not encouraged, because the only way the hoarder can make a profit is if a famine starts, and it would be evil for the hoarder to pray for a famine, which is what he would be motivated to do. Hoarding of food is totally prohibited during any shortages, and certainly during a famine.[*2]

Forging money is obviously a bad thing, but it is interesting to hear why Al-Ghazali thought it was bad. He was not worried about the intrusion on the ruler's monopoly on the production of money. What he was concerned about was that the forged coin would harm everybody in the community. It would circulate, and everyone who touched it would be damaged and hurt by its existence. This means that the entire community is hurt by the existence of a single forged coin.

Al-Ghazali also warned traders against creating a false market. He specifically warned against waiting at the gates of the market town, for the purpose of buying produce from farmers who had not yet been into town to study the market prices for themselves. It is also prohibited to exaggerate the qualities of a product that is for sale, to conceal defects, or to conceal anything about the price of a commodity. The sellers and buyers must be allowed access to the market. These comments were written nine centuries ago, but they are very pertinent to the capital markets of the present time.

Procedures for Change

The Holy books of religions tend to be very illiberal when it comes to market share issues, and the Quran is no exception. The fate which awaits those who, having been given the opportunity and an explanation, fail to appreciate and convert to the faith is painful in the extreme. Once past that hurdle, however, the Quran emphasises the lightness of the burden which it imposes on the believers. "God desires ease for you, not hardship for you" [Quran, 2:185]

In addition, the Quran places a very strong emphasis on freedom, to a greater degree (in the opinion of Goldziher, at least) than in the Hebrew or Christian Bibles. "He who forbids what is permitted is to be judged as he who declares the forbidden permissible", said Abdallah bin Masud, a Companion of the Prophet. When it is uncertain whether a thing should be declared forbidden or permissible, permission will prevail, because permission is the root. Everything is permitted, unless it has been specifically prohibited. [Goldziher, 1910, 56] This must surely be a very healthy approach to law-giving. The emphasis is on the individual to use his own sense of right and wrong to arrive at a decision on what to do, and the religious law is simply a codification of the actions which should be avoided.

The process for the collection of the hadiths has already been touched upon, and the role of Shafi'i as the great codifier has been discussed. There were other collectors of hadiths, notably Ahmad ibn Hanbal, who collected 80,000 of them and was founder of one of the other schools. The leaders of the other schools seem to have accepted the value of Shafi'i's work on tracing the roots of the hadith, and this has given Islam a very powerful unity. There is a hadith to the effect that "the differences of opinion among the learned of Islam is itself a sign of God's grace". The political fights that occurred as the Caliphate fell apart, and as secular power moved into the hands of dozens of local sultans, was not accompanied by a splintering of the church, which is what happened in the Christian world. The Islamic religious law held together, and more or less ignored the political fighting that was going on around it.

The concentration of the scholars of Sunni Islamic law into the four schools was accompanied by the evolution of a means of communication between them. The interpretive system of fiqh was used to enable the

71

various schools to give comparable verdicts to the same general class of secular and religion dispute, difference, or problem.

For the first three centuries of Islam there was a period of "creative interpretation", in which new ideas were being generated by a small but important group of innovative thinkers, who dealt with issues which the Prophet had never quite got around to. This had been a productive exercise, but it had obvious dangers, and the "ulama" the collective of Islamic thinkers, gradually formed three important doctrines. The first of these was the decision that the agreement of the ulama was the right way to arrive at doctrines. This doctrine of agreement, or ijma, was very controversial, but was adopted, and later refined as discussed by Goldziher.

"Ijma was defined as the concordant doctrines and opinions of those who are in any given period the acknowledged doctors of Islam. They are the men with power to bind and to loosen. It is their office to interpret and deduce law and theological doctrine. .... Clearly, this principle provides Islam with a potential for freedom of movement and a capacity for evolution." [Goldziher, 1910, 52]

The second doctrine was that there had been enough creative interpretation, and that the gate for new interpretations was to be deemed closed. This happened about 900AD. From then on, the third doctrine decreed, interpretations should be based on "imitation", so that there would be continuity of principle, though with a continuing need for up-to-date interpretation within those principles.

By these means, the doctrinal core of Islam is being continued to the present, subject to slow adjustment by means of fiqh, the consultative process among the Islamic legal schools. It should be made clear that the above discussion is almost entirely based on readings which concern the Sunni Islamic approach. The Shi'ite approach has not been considered at all.

Chapter Seven:- The Buddhist Tradition

Sizemore and Swearer organised a conference entitled "Ethics, Wealth, and Salvation:- A Study in Buddhist Social Ethics", and published the proceedings in 1990. The book is very largely devoted to expounding the Buddhist view on matters of business and economics, which is very helpful indeed. Accordingly, I have exploited this resource thoroughly. The extensive introduction by the editors is a valuable general resource, though they seem to be a bit too determined to make Buddhism fit their ideas of what it ought to mean. The papers by Green, Falk, and Rajavaramuni are valuable on special topics, and Rajavaramuni is an original source. The principal additional sources on Buddhism have been the Tibetan Dhammapada itself [Dharmatrata and Sparham 1986], and the writings of Rowley [1951] and of Rahula [1974].

In tackling financial ethics in a Buddhist context, the problem is unusually complicated by the fact that the sources do not seem to have considered the subject at all. I have searched carefully for a Buddhist view on lending, and have asked various people of great ability for guidance, but there does not seem to be one. Debt is accepted as a fact of life, and having too much debt is a very regrettable fact of life, but the writings of the religion do not seem to want to go beyond this. Instead, financial and commercial activity is seen as just another part of the routine activities of the laity, and no special consideration is deemed necessary.

That being the case, we have to begin by considering the writings of the Buddha for the guidance of the laity, and then to consider the nature of society and the virtues which the government will need to possess if a good situation is to be arrived at.

The fundamental principle of wealth in a Buddhist context is the principle of non-attachment. Pursuit of wealth is a perfectly worthy activity as long as you do not become concerned about that wealth. You may have riches, but you should be indifferent if they are lost. You may be poor, but you should not care about that either. To be non-attached is to possess and use material things but not to be possessed or used by them. This principle is repeated many times in the Dhammapada, and also in Rahula's book on the teachings of Buddha. [*6]

The main Buddhist teaching is that people should follow the Ariyan Eightfold Way, for which the Pali word is Magga. Rahula suggests that the entire teaching of Buddha is an amplification of that short list, and Rajavaramuni agrees that the Magga is uniquely important. The list is given below. He puts two prerequisites into the list, before the layman can start to work on the Eightfold Way, and these are called pre-magga by Rajavaramuni.

Pre-magga	Association with good people		
	Systematic reflection		
Magga	Wisdom	1	Right view
		2	Right thought
			Insight into impermanent, conflicting, nature of things, and concept that all change has a cause and has effect
	Morality	3	Right Speech
		4	Right Action
		5	Right Livelihood
			Socially responsible behaviour of each person to his society.
	Mental Discipline	6	Right Effort
		7	Right Mindfulness
		8	Right Concentration
			Developing mental qualities needed, earnestness, resolution, to follow path

[Phra Rajavaramuni, in Sizemore & Swearer, 1990, 47]

Neither layman nor monk can get started on the Eightfold Way unless they associate with good people, who will give them a helping hand in starting. Also, they are not going to get anywhere if they do not give the subject the concentrated attention and thought that it needs.

The next stage is to commence work on the three main tracks into which the Eightfold Way is divided; wisdom, morality, and mental discipline. There is no need here to go into these, except to touch on the fourth and fifth elements, Right Action and Right Livelihood. The details of this will be considered in the section on the legal framework.

There is no doubt that the Buddha envisaged a substantial reward for those who followed the Path. There is a chapter in the Dhammapada called "Ethics", and the spiritual satisfactions of the layman who has led a good life are clearly defined:- "Among seekers of the three happinesses:- the happiness of compliments, of getting wealth, and of an upper birth, those who are wise protect ethics. .... From ethics happiness is gained, there are no physical torments, at night a peaceful sleep, and happiness on waking up. Benevolent and ethical, with the merits from what they do, the wise always find happiness here and in the beyond. Ethics are a virtue even in old age, and to remain faithful is good. Wisdom is the jewel of the human race, and thieves find merit hard to steal." [Dharmatrata, Sparham, Gyatso, 1986, D,6,1-5]

This happy state can only be sought if the government has done its job of setting the scene for ethical prosperity. This task is extensively defined in the Buddhist writings, and Buddha wrote a long sermon on the qualities and virtues which kings were expected to have. "There are four sets of virtues and qualities that a Thai Buddhist king is supposed to possess, display, and encourage. The fourth set is called the five strengths of the monarch, of arms, of wealth, of ministers, of ancestry, and of wisdom. It is notable that poverty is not in any of the virtue lists. Poverty is regarded as the main source of crime, disorder, and greed. It is required of the ruler to make sure that there is a good accumulation of wealth and economic sufficiency, to ensure a happy, secure, stable society." {D.III.65: D.III.92} [Phra Rajavaramuni, in Sizemore & Swearer, 1990, 38]. Although the king is expected to ensure that there is prosperity, we shall see later that the king has no responsibility for redistribution of wealth under the Buddhist system.

Legal Principles of Justice and Restitution

The feature of Buddhism which differentiates it most from the other religions is the concept of retribution. This is not unique as a word, but is unique as a concept and in implementation. The doctrine of Kamma decrees that the citizen is invariably situated in exactly the situation he ought to be in. If you are in deep trouble, it is because you committed offences earlier. If you are in a very comfortable state, it is because you did glorious deeds at an earlier time, perhaps during a previous existence. The introduction to Sizemore and Swearer discusses the point thus:-

"There is a perfect harmony between virtue and prosperity. Whatever state you are in, you deserve to be there. However lowly, acts of virtue will be rewarded, however mighty, acts of vice will be punished. The law of kammic retribution ensures that justice has been done, whatever your state. Performing a meritorious action makes you deserving of a promotion of some sort, and also deserving of greater wealth. However, if you are leading a meritorious (dhammic) life for reasons of self-serving greed, the beneficial effect is lost." [Sizemore and Swearer, 1990, 4]

To western ears, this sounds a rather bizarre arrangement. If I am in some sort of trouble, I am apparently expected by the Buddhists to put the blame for this on sins I know I have committed, which is fair enough, but also sins I have committed in a previous incarnation, which I can remember absolutely nothing about. The concept, however, needs to be examined more completely. Consider the following, from the S&S introduction.

"The doctrine of kammic retribution is an exceptionless moral justification for the existing distribution of wealth. Buddhists interested in more even distributions cannot appeal to moral desert, only to the principle of non-attachment, and the virtues of generosity and compassion." [Sizemore and Swearer, 1990, 12]

It is therefore a matter of persuading the rich to give to the poor, to feed the poor, or alternatively of persuading the rich to give to the sangha (=priesthood) who will pass it on. The option of redistributive taxation is not open. S&S draw attention to a remark of Rajavaramuni on this point, in the following terms. [*1,9]

"There is a basic moral equality over all the social lines. There are rich and poor donors, men and women, free and slave. The law of kammic retribution applies to all, and promotions and demotions take effect from wherever you started from. Rajavaramuni says the only thing that matters is the way you got wealth and the way you spend it, so the state has no role in dealing with distributional matters. It is not the job of the state to make things equal." [Sizemore and Swearer, 1990, 21]

For westerners, brought up on the tale of the Good Samaritan and others of similar import, this is definitely "new news". Also, the taxation systems of most western countries are designed to redistribute the total national income, as one of their several objectives. S&S comment on the specific issue of helping the less fortunate in this manner.

"If all beings deserve their present fates, why should anyone act to change anything? The man the Good Samaritan helped deserved to be in the ditch. But to help him is still a meritorious action. And, although he deserved to be in the ditch, he also deserved to be helped. The virtue of compassion imposes an obligation on the passerby, not any sense of justice. Insofar as it was a costly action, the concept of non-attachment also bears on the helper's decision to help." [Sizemore and Swearer, 1990, 12][*13]

The Buddhist system does not, therefore, rely on the concept of restitution, by legal disputation followed by a judgement in some kind of court. Instead, the Buddhist system relies on a positive motivation to persuade people to engage in morally positive actions, by offering higher and higher status to those who engage in them. These improvements in status may take place during one's present life, and will usually include substantial prosperity. Alternatively, or in addition, the improvements may affect the agent during a subsequent incarnation, steadily improving his situation until the ultimate state of nibbana (sometimes written 'nirvana') is attained.

Up to this point, the main topic has been very individual. It is necessary now to consider the Buddhist legal scheme as it affects and creates societies. There are two different but parallel systems of training in Buddhism, one for the monks and one for the laity. It is very common for young men to become trainee monks for a couple of years, so that they acquire a good knowledge of the lay training and a fairly good understanding of the basics of the monks' training too. Rajavaramuni explains that "For the lay person, the main Buddhist teaching concentrates on dana (charity), on morality (sila), and on mental development. The mission of this training is to help lay people to build good social relationships and to engage in more concrete actions." [Phra Rajavaramuni, in Sizemore & Swearer, 1990, 49]

We will consider charity in the next segment, and morality in the segment on wealth and general management. The mental development which is sought in the training of the laity is, as far as economic issues are concerned, very much a matter of learning non-attachment and patience. There are also important lessons about community development and the special role of the rulers.

There are parallels between the doctrine of non-attachment and the views of the other religions about wealth. There is nothing wrong with being rich, they all say, provided you obtained the wealth by appropriately fair means and that you use it for appropriate purposes, one of which will always be to look after your own family. The objectionable part of wealth is becoming attached to it, or hoarding. Getting so concerned about losing your wealth that you cease to be involved in doing normal civic duties and involvements because you are spending so much time on protecting your assets. In Buddhism, there are numerous stories, which might be thought comparable to the parables in the Christian tradition, in which the life of a person is described. In a large number of these, the hero is rich, then uses his wealth to fight an oppressive adversary, and then regains his wealth after winning that fight. Most of these stories end with the hero renouncing his new wealth and entering the priesthood, when he realises that the wealth is totally unimportant in comparison with spiritual advancement. This is recited in the Dhammapada in the chapter on craving in the following terms. "To Buddhas and Hearers who take no pleasure in even the objects that the gods desire, the end of craving gives pleasure. They understand that even a heap of gold as big as a high snow mountain cannot satisfy even one person, and therefore conduct themselves well." [Dharmatrata, Sparham, Gyatso, 1986, D,2,18][*6,2]

The retribution which follows displays of human greed for sense pleasures and material satisfaction, and especially the hoarding of wealth, is raised by several of the authors in the Sizemore and Swearer compendium, usually in quite similar terms. "The gathering of wealth by appropriate methods is perfectly acceptable. However, wealth becomes a hindrance when it generates the craving that perpetuates human suffering, but it is a positive good when used for the proper purposes of giving to the Buddha's community, and when the gift is made with the proper attitude, which means to give joyfully, selflessly, without stinting" [Falk, in S&S, 124] "The storied donors occupy every conceivable station in life....... All give whatever they can, and they give without clinging. They may contemplate the benefit their gift will accomplish for others, but they preferably show no interest in its potential fruits for themselves...." [Falk, 142][*2]. Green, also in S&S, discusses the Buddhist book of Genesis, the Agganna Suttanta, in which various attempts at hoarding were severely punished. Not by God, as there is no God in Buddhism to do this, but because greed is its own undoing. "Disordered self assertion diminishes nature's abundance and corrupts the human body, promotes strife, and makes a fierce government necessary. .... there is a passage in the Agganna Suttanta which describes how some people tried to hoard rice, only to find that the hoarded rice went bad and would not seed. A close parallel is to be found in the Jewish story about how families were punished for trying to hoard manna in the desert. Those who try to buttress their positions by acquisitiveness wind up undermining their own positions and may jeapordise the welfare of the whole community" [Green, in S&S, 230] [*2]

Attachment to wealth is unequivocally condemned, and, at the other end of the economic scale, the problems of poverty are condemned too. Buddhism does not recommend poverty for any purpose. Extreme scarcity, at the level which stimulates crime and serious greed, is an unreservedly bad thing. However, above that level, the Buddhist is expected to be content with what he has, and not to feel upset that others are richer. His attitude must be one of patience in adversity, and of undertaking good actions in hope of a blessing, which may take the form of an increase in wealth or it may turn out to be something else.

Patience in suffering and adversity is a major feature of the writings of the Buddha and of his disciples. Coping with loss and tragedy is a major topic, but these losses are not, usually, economic ones. The assumption is that an economic loss is of no concern to a properly non-attached Buddhist. Other personal losses are much more serious and more sympathetically handled. "A woman who had lost her husband and children in an accident sought solace from the Buddha in her grief, but he could not console her. So he sent her to go round the city and ask each house that had not suffered a death to give her a mustard seed for Buddha's use. There were no houses which had not suffered. She returned to Buddha empty-handed, but reconciled to her loss. The Dhammapada is a major source of discussion about the issue of suffering and how patience in adversity is a sign of Brahmin stature." [Rowley, 1951, 33]

The role of government in the legal system is important in Buddhism as it is everywhere. The comments of Buddha on what the king should be doing in the field of economics is very enlightening and extremely modern. "The Buddha suggests that in order to eradicate crime the economic conditions of the people should be improved. The king should provide grain and equipment for the farmers. Capital should be provided to get the traders working. The wage rates should be adequate for modest living. In this way, the country will be at least fairly prosperous and crime free." [Rahula, 1974, 82]   This approach to government stimulation of the economy through increasing public sector purchasing and promoting high wage rates to enable the workers to take part in the more advanced elements of economic life was re-invented by Prof J

Maynard Keynes about 2550 years after Buddha first suggested it. It is rather sad that we lost it for most of the period in between. [*4,1]

Assuming the king does his bit, the economy should perform reasonably well, and the resulting prosperity will enable the crime rate to be held down, may keep the king in office, and should permit a certain amount of leisure for spiritual contemplation. The quality of the society is a function of this, and is the summation of the virtue of all of its members. As each member of a society influences the others for good or for ill, he will reap the reward of living in the society which results from their efforts and his own.

Charitable Actions

The wealth of the rich is assumed in Buddhist thinking of the Theravada persuasion to have arisen because of a previous demonstration of non-attachment and previous and current meritorious actions. An earlier renunciation of wealth, coupled with generous charitable donations, would be rewarded in numerous ways, but one of these might be a new major accretion of wealth.

One of the major characters of Buddhism, a contemporary of the Gautama Buddha, was a banker. His true name was Sudatta, but the Buddha gave him the name and title of Anathapindika {"he who gives food to the poor and the powerless"}. Anathapindika was a rather colourful personage as bankers go, and made several enormous fortunes, lost some of them, renounced some of the others, and gave Buddha enough money to built a vast monastery, the Jetavana at Savathi. When the land for the monastery was being negotiated for purchase, and the seller was proving reluctant, Anathapindika is alleged to have covered the desired territory with gold bricks, as his final offer. The seller, Prince Jeta, was so stunned by this that he too became a disciple of Buddha, and asked to be allowed to donate some of the land for the monastery.

The Buddha's comments on business and economics are largely contained in his conversations with Anathapindika, and also with a young pupil named Sigala, who seems to have been engaged in a business startup and wanted advice on how to do it ethically. These comments are, of course, additional to the pre-Keynesian sermon to the king mentioned earlier.

"The Buddha told Anathapindika, the great banker, that a layman has four kinds of happiness. First, economic security from wealth justly obtained. Second, spending liberally on self, family, friends, and meritorious deeds. Third, to be free from debt. The fourth happiness, worth more than sixteen times the others, is the spiritual happiness of living a pure and faultless life." [Rahula, 1974, 83]

The first three of these are straightforward benefits accruing to the laity, and presumably not easily available to the monks, because the layman is able to spend time earning and trading while the monks have the higher duties of prayer and contemplation, which are not cash-generating in normal circumstances. In the fourth happiness, however, the vastly greater value of spiritual happiness is emphasised. This is accessible to everyone, but it is more easily accessed by the priests.

It has been mentioned above that the Buddhist scheme does not allow for governmental redistribution of wealth. Instead, the task of redistribution depends on the concept of non-attachment, under which the current holders of wealth appreciate the impermanence of it, the unimportance of it, and take action. The giving of charity to the poor is highly meritorious, and the giving of charity to the priesthood, which is called dana, is even more meritorious. Also, the complicated rules governing dana enabled the poor and the rich to have comparable access to the merit which both are seeking. [*1,9]

S&S discuss this topic in their introduction and point to the importance of the thinking behind each gift and the merit of the recipient as important determinants of the merit gained by the donor. They make four points about dana:- "[1] Dana is consistent with the denial of craving. The "field of merit" is the description of the recipient, and the higher the field of merit the more credit the donor is awarded. A gift to an especially highly respected monk would count highly. [2] Dana emphasises the orientation one has towards wealth. The "efficiency of the thought" is a measure of the extent to which the donor is non-attached. So you can get a big merit by giving anything, however tiny, to a high field of merit with an efficient thought. This means the poor can gain merit, almost as easily as the rich. [3] Dana is a way for laymen to show that they understand the provisional value of prosperity. Wealth used appropriately is meritorious to the whole community. [4] Material wealth is only provisional. Spiritual wealth is far more important. [Sizemore and Swearer, 1990, 14]

In general, the Buddhist thinking on charity seems to place great emphasis upon method and on motive, and relatively little on amount. The emphasis is to ensure that the layman obtained the funds in a fair and legitimate fashion. Then, the layman is expected to remain non-attached to the wealth, and to have good thoughts and intentions as to how he can do good for his community. Lastly, the layman is expected to implement these good thoughts and intentions in cash. [*10]

Lending

I have not been able to find any discussion whatever about debt in the books I have studied on Buddhism, so far. There is nothing prohibiting, nor indeed advocating usury. There is no comment on the problems of obtaining repayment for a debt. There are secular laws in Thailand and in China about these matters, but I have found nothing in the Dhammapada or in Rahula's survey of the Buddha's sayings.

Debt is mentioned, for instance in the sermon to Anathapindika, as a state to be avoided, or at least to be exited from as rapidly as feasible. It is not classed as a state to be avoided at all costs, nor is the lender mentioned as behaving in any way reprehensibly in making the loan. Interest rates are not discussed.

This relaxed attitude to debt is compatible with a similarly relaxed approach to property ownership in the essay by Rajavaramuni. As debt and property ownership are regularly joined together, it may be legitimate to assume that the Buddhist approach to debt is also tranquil. "In Buddhist ethics, wealth is only a means, not an end. It is a question not of the polarities of wealth and poverty, but of how to deal with wealth and when to be independent of or freed from wealth. As long and as far as wealth is necessary as a resource, it should be used for achieving social well-being and thus for providing favourable circumstances for the individual development of all members of the society. As long as wealth is used in this way, it does not matter to whom it belongs, whether the individual, the community, or the society. Wealth can rightfully be personal as long as the wealthy person acts as a provider or resource of wealth for the society, or as a field where wealth grows for the benefit of one's fellows. Without such a value, wealth is useless, the wealthy man is worthless, and the accumulation of wealth becomes evil." [Phra Rajavaramuni, in Sizemore & Swearer, 1990, 53][*7,10,13]

It all sounds wonderfully peaceful, compared to the fights which seem to surround the average debt contract in the western world. Perhaps it really is like that. Or perhaps I have just been looking in the wrong sources.

Please take note of a very fascinating line in the quote from Rajavaramuni above. Wealth can rightfully be personal ...... if the wealthy person acts as a provider .... or as a field where wealth grows for the benefit of one's fellows ..... This is a fascinating phrase. If the writer is quoting an old text, it would seem to imply that the investment management industry is a lot older than I had imagined. Even if it is recent it sheds an interesting new light on the job.

Wealth and General Management

The ethical instructions of Buddhism for the monks and for the laity are very different and are clearly separated. The assignments for the lay people from Buddha are the following. You should seek wealth lawfully and unarbitrarily. You should make yourself happy and cheerful. You should share with others and do meritorious deeds. You should make use of your wealth without greed and longing, and without infatuation. [Phra Rajavaramuni, in Sizemore & Swearer, 1990, 45]

These orders are clearly consistent with the concept of non-attachment. It is perfectly all right to get rich as long as you do not allow your riches to take over your life.

The basic thrust of Theravada Buddhism on wealth is captured in the four commands. [a] Craving is bad, and implies ignorance of the true nature of the self. [b] Wealth, in the absence of craving, is good. [c] Wealth is a sign of virtue. Kamma guarantees a fate based upon deserving. However, [d] At the higher levels of virtue and wisdom, wealth is recognised as meaningless. The salvation of the individual soul at that level is recognized to be so vastly more important that wealth is just not important at all. [Sizemore and Swearer, 1990, 6]

When it comes down to the daily life of the merchants, the workers, and the bankers in the community, the instructions of the Buddha are contained in the eight virtues. These are the four virtues which lead to temporal welfare and the four virtues which lead to prosperity. These eight virtues were expounded by Buddha in two sermons, as well as being in the Dhammapada itself. The four virtues which lead to temporal welfare are [a] To be endowed with energy, industry, and skill in management. [b] To be endowed with attentiveness. [c] To associate with good people. And [d] To have a balanced livelihood {A.IV.281}. The four virtues which lead to prosperity are [e] To live in a good environment. [f] To associate with good people. [g] To aspire and direct oneself in the right way. [h] To have prepared oneself studiously and by deep thinking so as to create a good background. {D.III.276: A.II.32} [Phra Rajavaramuni, in Sizemore & Swearer, 1990, 38]

It is interesting that the Buddha included "skill in management" as a virtue which would lead to temporal welfare. It certainly is not a surprise to us now, 2600 years on. It is interesting though, that the existence of the concept called "skill in management" was available to the Buddha at that time. Or, alternatively, it is interesting that he promulgated the concept, but that nobody took it up for about twenty five centuries.

Further guidance to the laity is offered in the Ariyan Eightfold Way, and this includes some ideas about the conduct of one's business life. First of all, under the fifth chapter, the "right livelihood", certain jobs are simply prohibited to Buddhist people. These include arms trading, trading in alcohol or poison, jobs which require cheating and misinformation, and jobs that involve killing any animals. [*8]

In addition to this guidance, the Buddha gave very specific ideas on how to run a company in a more detailed sermon, the Sigala-sutta [Digha-Nikaya 31], in which, inter alia, he talks about relationships with employees. The employer must assign work according to ability and capacity. Adequate wages should be paid. Medical needs should be provided. Occasional bonuses should be granted. The employee should be diligent and not lazy, honest and obedient and not cheat his employer, and should be earnest in his work. [Rahula, 1974, 47 & 80][*3,4]

This is really rather modern thinking. The Sigala-sutta makes it clear that employment is a two-way contract. The employer has a list of duties, and the employee has a list of duties, and each of them is obliged to work on that basis. The concept that the employer must assign work according to ability and capacity must have been quite revolutionary at the time. The practice had always been to give jobs to relations. The idea of paying bonuses was commonplace in the earliest times, but the idea of paying "adequate" wages was also a revolutionary idea, as was the concept of providing medical care. BUPA, for instance, has been around for less than a century.

To conclude this section on wealth and general management it may be suitable to quote a verse from the Dhammapada, from the chapter called "Actions". "Do not do the bad actions you discover that others do - do not do those things. The wrongs you do will follow you. Extremely violent acts, deceit, and swindling on weight and bulk, doing harm to other beings, and inciting others to these wrongs. The consequences of these actions hurl the one who does them from the cliff." [Dharmatrata, Sparham, Gyatso, 1986, D,9,6]   This general command is interestingly formulated. The reader is expected to be able to be his own judge to determine whether the observed actions of other people are or are not worthy of emulation. He is not, at least in this text, expected to call in expert advice. He is supposed to work it out for himself. In a country with as many monks as most Buddhist countries possess, he will certainly have guidance available if he needs it; at the same time the obligation to decide remains with the actor. [*3]

Procedures for Change

The Buddhist approach to changing their own rules in the light of new technology or new social norms or other new factors is materially different from the procedures for change in the other religions. The totality of Buddhist thinking is contained in the Eightfold Way and its prerequisites. At the same time, there is a clear distinction drawn between the different sets of documents and how each of these can be adapted.

The whole of Buddhist ethics is contained in the dhamma, which contains the principles and the ideals of Buddhism, and the vinaya, which contains the discipline, the rules and regulations which make the rules firm and clear.   Also, there is a completely different set of standards for the monks from those which apply to the laity. A book published in about 450AD called the Visuddhimagga contains the principles and the rules as they apply to the monks, and this book is still "in force" as a regulating document. This does not apply to the laity, however, and the vinaya for the laity is a much more adaptable affair, as Rajavaramuni explains:- "The vinaya (discipline) for the monks has been fixed and rather closed, but that for the laity is to a large extent left open for temporal regulation to suit the specific time or place. The vinaya for the monks was laid down by Buddha. The vinaya for the laity is left open for able and righteous people, like enlightened monarchs, to formulate based on the general ideas and principles enunciated by the

Buddha. In principle, this lay vinaya should enjoin the kind of social organisation that maintains a society of good friends in which people live together for the mutual benefit, where all environmental conditions are favourable to the individual development and perfection" [Phra Rajavaramuni, in Sizemore & Swearer, 1990, 49][*10]

It follows that the Buddhist layman or woman has a much greater responsibility for the decision on what is ethical and what is not than a Jew or a Christian, and even than a Moslem. Buddhism sets forth the middle way, tells you to avoid excessive sensuality and to avoid excessive asceticism, and then lets you get on with it. This individual responsibility, within the regulations set by the community in which one is living, has a considerable amount in common with Protestant Christianity, but may be even more individually demanding.

In his discussion of the issue of motivation and responsibility, Rajavaramuni makes the individual's role in the matter completely clear. "The first and good kind (of motivation) is dhamma-chanda, desire for good and to do good. The other is akusala-chanda, the desire for indulgence and to gratify the self. The Buddhist must take time to study his own actions, to see which is in operation, and to promote dhamma-chanda and restrain indulgence. [Phra Rajavaramuni, in Sizemore & Swearer, 1990, 51]

The adaptation of these rules over time would appear to have the potential to become unbounded. There would seem to be no controls at all, except what the local authorities chose to introduce. It would seem that the stability of the system depends on the rigidity of the vinaya for the monks, and on the continuous interaction between monks and laity, so that the latter may be reminded continually of the merits and demerits of the two varieties of motivation, and of the nature of dhamma.

Chapter Eight:- An Aggregation of the Commands from the Religions

If the reader has worked through the last four chapters, it must have become obvious that the commands of the various religious founders and leaders on the business topics covered are quite alike. The secondary reference markers [*1] to [*13] have indicated the points in the discussions where the following requirements are to be found in each of the four religious chapters.

The Uniform Requirements

First of all, we may list the commands that are indistinguishably similar, as these may be adopted without argument.

[1]   All of the religions make it clear that it is essential that their adherents should make provision for the poor. In some instances, the amount to be given is specified, but in all cases the expectation is made clear that the rich adherent should make large donations and that the less rich adherents should make lesser ones. It is also made clear that there is no merit in making such large charitable donations that the adherent impoverishes himself, because then he has failed to protect his own family, who ought to be the first beneficiaries of his care.

[2]   There is a general prohibition of hoarding, especially of food. The idea here is that the adherent is not allowed to buy a commodity and put it aside until the price goes up if there are people who need that commodity for their basic living now.

[3]   All adherents are required to make use of scales, weights, and other measures which are correct and accurate.

[4]   Adherents are required to pay wages which are fair to the employees, and these fair wages are not to be oppressively low.

[5]   If the adherent is a trustee for the assets of a juvenile, then the trustee must never divert the trust funds to his own use.

[6]   It is perfectly acceptable for the adherent to be rich, provided the adherent does not become obsessed with money. Being rich enables you do many good things which you could not do without the funds. All the

religions instruct their rich adherents to be very careful and watchful that they do not become ensnared by their own bank balances.

[7]   It is normal and desirable that at least some adherents should engage in business as partners, sharing in the prosperity and sharing also if there is a loss. These business ventures make the whole community better off, as long as the venture is not engaged in evil actions.

The General Requirements

It is also possible for us to list those instructions to adherents which were not issued, specifically, by all four of the religions, but which were issued by at least two in specific terms and were either implicitly supported or ignored by the other two. If any instruction was given by two sources, but something like its opposite was issued by one other, then that instruction would not appear in this group.

[8]   Giving false evidence under oath is specifically condemned by the three monotheistic religions. Buddhism, which has an apparent preference for giving positive instructions rather than prohibitions, points to honesty as one of the many paths that may lead to a higher rebirth.

[9]   There is a positive obligation to support the clergy in Buddhism and Islam. This support, which is normally financial but can take other forms, is also expected in Christianity, though the expectation has now become implicit, in place of the former tithe arrangements. The precise amount of the help expected is defined in Judaism, according to a formula based on the division of the crop from a field. It is perhaps not surprising that there is unanimity amongst the religions concerning the need to give cash or equivalent to the clergy. The clergy write the regulations.

[10] There is a positive requirement to sustain the community or the society in the four religions studied. These requirements are not exactly similar, but they have a family resemblance. Maududi observed that the private wealth of Islamic adherents was a positive feature if it was used for the service of virtue and the welfare of the public. Rajavaramuni states that the private possession of wealth is perfectly reasonable, if the Buddhist owner serves as a "field" in which the wealth can grow for the benefit of the community at large. Calvin observed that riches provided a hazard for the rich Christian, but that they could avoid the hazard if they gave most of it away for good causes. In the book of Timothy

[1,6,17-19], we find the instruction "Charge them that are rich in this world. .... that they do good, that they be rich in good works, ready to distribute, willing to communicate...". In the Hebrew Bible, especially in Psalms and Ecclesiastes, the Jew who finds himself getting rich is instructed not to set his heart upon it, and not to take his new wealth too seriously. Very specific rules are laid down concerning the amounts to be donated by each Jew to the rabbinate, and similarly strict regulations govern the ways in which the rabbis are to recycle these funds to the benefit of the lesser folk of the community.

The Points of Difference

There are, obviously, points of detail about which the religions differ in terms of business guidance. At the same time, it has to be said that there are very few points of difference of any importance. I have found only three.

[11]   The treatment of interest is one of the most interesting differences among the four religions. The Moslems have banned interest ever since they started. The Buddhists regard interest with more or less complete indifference, as being a fact of life which can be a problem if you are paying too much of it, but about which the religion has no strong opinions. The Jews are under orders to charge interest to all Gentiles, and equally under orders to charge none to other Jews. The Christians banned interest from about 300AD until about 1550AD, but adopted the concept for pragmatic reasons from then on. The basic objection to interest is that it is effortless. All a lender has to do to earn his interest payment is to grow older. He is indifferent as to whether the venture he lent to is doing well or poorly, as long as it achieves the minimal success required to repay his loan. The basic argument for interest is that it may persuade cautious people who have money to put their cash to work, bringing added prosperity to the community. The less cautious, under this theory, will already have invested in partnerships and other forms of equity interest.

[12]   Each of the religions has some set of rules for dealing with business mishap. They vary in detail, but have certain common features. Assuming the person whose firm has failed has not been crooked, Islam and Judaism categorically state that he should be allowed to keep his house and his toolbox and a reasonable amount of furniture. Christianity and Buddhism each possess some writers who regard wealth as an

indicator of merit and poverty as an indication of its absence. The kammic distribution law is explicit on this. The Christian habit of jailing bankrupts until a century ago is a less precise but still quite convincingly different approach to this problem area. More recently, the Christians have adopted regulations which are very like the original Jewish and Islamic ones. A Buddhist is expected to regard the loss of his money with indifference; presumably if you lend to someone else, and he loses your money for you, a similarly tranquil reaction is called for.

[13] There is a substantial difference between the religions on the topic of duty, especially with regard to giving aid. Judaism is quite clear on the matter. There is a very strong obligation to provide all the assistance which you can provide to your near relatives, and this obligation falls away as the people become less connected to the potential helper. Buddhism and Christianity are rather alike in the policy adopted on aid, though for different reasons. The Good Samaritan rule obliges Christians to give assistance to those who need assistance, purely because they need it, and not because of any pre-existing contract (a blood relationship, however distant, would be a contract in this situation). The Buddhist would be always on the lookout for opportunities to engage in meritorious conduct, which would be recorded to his credit and would tend to produce a reward, either in the present life or in the form of an advantageous rebirth next time. The second sura of the Quran gives an instruction about aid which is very broadly defined. "True piety is this: to believe in God, in the Last Day, the angels, the Book, and the Prophets, to give of one's substance, however cherished, to kinsmen, and orphans, the needy, the traveller, beggars, and to ransom the slave. To perform the prayer, to pay the alms, and fulfil any covenant they have signed." The important difference between the religions on this topic is the definition of the recipients to be served. Should it be kin, or should it be everybody? From the texts shown here, it seems that the majority vote on the duty to give aid would be to offer it to everyone who is in need. The texts of Islam, Buddhism, and Judaism would place relatives firmly at the front of the queue, however, and Christians adopt a similar policy as a matter of practice.

Discussion of the Points of Difference

Interest is a point of difference of great importance. The reasoning used by the early Christians to ban interest was quite similar to the arguments by the Islamic community, historically and today. This has already been discussed in the Islamic chapter above. The interest payment is not "earned" by the lender, whereas a person who puts in money as a sleeping partner does earn his reward by sharing in the risk. A modern banker would argue that he does in fact take a risk when he lends, but would admit that the risk is less than a shareholder assumes. Over the centuries, there have been efforts made time and time again to stop the lending of money at interest, and these efforts have regularly failed.

The arguments in favour of interest are mainly economic. There is a class of investment opportunities which are so attractive that everybody wants to take part as a shareholder, and there is no need for debt capital to get this economic benefit to the community up and running. There is another class of investment opportunities which are so hazardous, or otherwise so unattractive, that nobody wants to be a part of it at all, and the only way the economic benefits to the community will be achieved is if a single investor is willing to take a big gamble. In between these extremes, there is a broad range of projects which have the potential to bring community benefit. The capital required will be raised normally by appealing to a broad range of people, ranging from those who are financially cautious to those who are financially fairly adventurous. In order to raise enough capital for these projects, it makes sense to try to appeal to the cautious, to the adventurous, and to those whose attitudes to risk lie between the other two groups. More economic benefit will accrue to the community if more projects can be commenced, and that means attracting capital from all those who have it. Attracting money from the cautious normally involves allowing them to invest in loan capital on a fixed interest basis.

The decision on whether interest should be allowed therefore rests on a balance between two good results. Allowing interest will cause more projects to happen, and this in turn will result in a more prosperous community. Prohibiting interest will reduce the amount of economic activity in the community, but will also eliminate the distress caused on those infrequent occasions when a lender forcibly (in the bankruptcy courts) reclaims his capital from a failing entrepreneur and his family. Modern bankruptcy law is a very much less traumatic affair than it used to be, however. The ridiculous procedure of jailing a bankrupt was only abandoned in Britain in 1869, but it has gone now, and the doctrine of a fresh start after all inessential assets have been sold for the creditors is virtually universal. Bankruptcy is still stressful for all concerned; this difficulty is alleviated (when considered from a nationwide viewpoint) by the relative leniency of the revised law, and by the relative rarity of its occurrence in modern times.

At present (1999), there is a comparable controversy about bankruptcy of countries. There are several countries whose debts are such, and whose income is such, that, if they were people, they would have been declared bankrupt long ago. We do not have a mechanism for dealing adequately with this on a national level. None of the religions seem to have clearcut pronouncements on this in their formative writings. The widely publicised "Jubilee" project, which asks the big creditors to write off debts to the poorest nations, is a very well-meant attempt to deal with the matter. It certainly has made a lot of people more aware of the problem. There seem to be rather a lot of unrealistic expectations, both among the creditors and the supporters of the debtors, unfortunately. It seems rather important that the World Bank and other creditors should appreciate that their loans to the poorest countries are already lost. Leaving these loans on the creditors books, even at a written-down value, is false accounting, and claims an asset which no auditor should allow them to show.

In more normal situations, I really think debt capital does considerably more good than harm. However I also think there is room for another kind of capital, the redeemable ordinary share, which might better meet the needs of the cautious investor and the nervous entrepreneur. This will be discussed in a later chapter.

The remaining topic is duty, and especially the duty to provide assistance. It is obviously not controversial that someone who sees another in trouble and gives appropriate assistance is worthy of praise. The problem is whether there is a moral <u>obligation</u> to provide that assistance.

The parable of the Good Samaritan in Luke Chapter ten is an important part of the Christian policy on this topic. A lawyer had observed that the moral law of the time required those who sought heaven to "love their neighbour as themselves", and he asked Jesus who his neighbour was. A man was mugged on the Jericho road, and left half dead with no clothes or money. A priest and a levite walked right past him, and a Samaritan gave him first aid and paid for his hotel room. The Samaritan was clearly the neighbour. From this it would appear that merit accrues to the Samaritan under the Christian rules, purely because of the spontaneous helpful action. The parable makes it fairly clear that there was no contract between the Samaritan and the thieves' victim, nor were they related in any way. There was therefore no implicit contract of mutual assistance between them. By extension, it would appear that the Christian is expected to give help to anyone who is in difficulties, solely because they are in difficulties.

The Islamic and Jewish rules on this matter are quite alike, and are much more restricted. There is a clear obligation to help kinsmen who are in trouble. There is a general obligation to help the poor. It is clear, however, that there is a definite hierarchy of helpfulness, in which you have a very great obligation to help relatives, a substantial obligation to help fellow-members of the community, a moderate obligation to help fellow-countrymen, and so on in a descending scale. It is not clear whether this descending scale ever reaches the zero point, but the obligation to help clearly becomes a very weak force indeed in the case of total strangers.

It is fairly clear, as a matter of crude observation, that the majority of people, whatever their religion or lack of one, seem to be following the Jewish/Islamic rule. Blood is indeed thicker than water. While many Jewish people and many Moslems would, as a practical matter, give aid to the man who was mugged in the same manner as the Samaritan did, they would tend to reject the suggestion that they were under an obligation to do so, or that it was a duty. Quite a few Christians, dare I suggest, might feel the same way, because of an imperfect understanding of the parable's very tough message.

In the financial community, of course, people get "mugged" in a host of ways which are financially, not physically, painful. The common consequence is that the victim is in need of financial aid. It seems clear that all the religions would agree that the victim's relatives have an obligation to assist him. The religions disagree on whether anybody else has such an obligation. As one who was brought up in a Presbyterian manse, I regret that I have to report that I can see no justification for the Samaritan rule to apply here. If someone goes broke, I do not have an obligation to help him financially unless there was a pre-existing "contract". This contract could be a normal legal one, but would more probably be the implicit kind which arises from a blood relationship, from living next door, from being a member of the same organisation, and generally from being a fellow member of some community of reasonable personal importance. Most societies now provide some kind of "safety net" against the most serious consequences of financial bankruptcy, and I fully accept the need for every citizen to pay a share of the cost of creating such a safety net for the future benefit of non-criminal bankrupts.

Chapter Nine:- The Remaining Task. The Commands we have Yet to Fulfil

In the previous chapters of this part, we have looked at the commands of the four religions and have produced a consolidated set of instructions. The task of the present chapter is to take a long hard look at these instructions and work out which of them we (or our predecessors) have already dealt with, which are current business, and which we have been ignoring and therefore need to re-focus upon

Perhaps the religions may take some satisfaction from the ease with which the modern financial person [MFP] could agree to many of the instructions. Some of them are so widely accepted that they hardly need to be stated.

The Easy Instructions

About half of the instructions from the religions seem to be very easy for the modern financial person to agree to. In several instances, the instructions have been, in a sense, over-ridden by the increased role of local and national government. In other cases, the modern legal system has supported the religions so thoroughly that the MFP does not realise the instruction originally came from a religious source.

Giving to the poor is a charitable religious action which has been nationalised. The religions are unanimous about its importance, but most governments have taken action so that it is no longer an optional action. The tax system, in all the developed (OECD) countries, takes about 40% of each country's GDP into the Treasury. About a quarter of this, or ten per cent of GDP, is then recycled in various ways for the benefit of those deemed poor enough to be deserving.

The order that we are to use fair weights and measures has been embedded in legislation from the earliest days of parliament. The instruction that we should not expropriate the trust assets of a minor is almost as long-lived. The instruction that fair wages should be paid which are not oppressively low has been adopted as a government action also, though in this case the initiative came from the embryonic union movement, and continues to receive emphasis from the movement in its mature form. The instruction about wages is fairly well handled within each country; it is quite a different story when we come to consider international comparisons.

The bankruptcy laws in the UK have been a shameful chapter in our history. We had perfectly adequate guidance from Judaism (about 200AD) and from Islam (about 900AD) on how to handle this problem. It is only a little less than a century and half back from the present that we managed to catch up and treat bankrupts in a more or less civilised fashion. It would be an interesting book for someone to write, to explain why we were so bad at dealing with this problem. This book is not the place to do it. At the present time, with a new millenium in sight, we can report that the problem has, at long last, been dealt with. Bankrupts are punished by losing the possessions they do not really need, not by taking away the items which constitute their only hope of recovery.

In a different manner, it would, I think, be fair to claim that the requirement to avoid false testimony and false oaths has also been sufficiently dealt with. We have perjury laws to deal with the matter if it appears in court, and we have newshounds who claim to be able to deal with false reports in parliament. In the stock market, someone who "welched" on a deal would rapidly lose the confidence of the other traders. The offence of false testimony continues to be committed, but the remedies in place are reasonably good. If they were much more stringent than they are now, we would perhaps find ourselves punishing people for honest errors in testimony, and that could cause people to be unwilling to give evidence at all. This is already a problem in some areas of criminal law.

The instructions of the religions as listed above have been assimilated so thoroughly into our national thinking, and indeed into the national thinking of most of the other OECD countries, that we do not need to be told that they are the right way to behave. There are, of course, a few who act contrary to these precepts. There have been such people since Abraham was a youth. Nonetheless, these items are simply not controversial now, and we will spend no time upon them. Of the list in chapter eight, the ones which have been dealt with are numbers 1,3,4,5,8,and 12.

The Tricky Items

The remaining instructions from the four religions have not been resolved. These instructions, usually given quite clearly in the original religious texts, remain issues to which the MFP would have difficulty in conforming, at least in the fullest sense. A few of them are currrently receiving the attention of the capital market authorities, but most of them are simply not being addressed at all. These topics are the following, using the numbers from chapter eight:-

[2]   Hoarding is sinful, especially of necessities like food. This is usually handled well enough as far as food is concerned in the developed countries, but is definitely a remaining issue with respect to other commodities and with respect to food in the developing countries, especially the poorest of them. It is also a remaining issue with regard to money itself

[3]   The employee should be paid wages which are not oppressively low. This is generally handled fairly well at the national level, and appallingly badly at the international level. Income ranges have been the subject of many studies, notably by the OECD [Smeeding et al 1995] and by the World Bank [1995a, 1995b]. The normal measure of range is to divide the population of interest into ten groups from richest to poorest, and to define the range by dividing the income of the people at the 90% mark by the income of the people at the 10% mark. Smeeding found the range in Finland to be the smallest, about three, and the range in the USA to be the largest, about eight. The ratio of the highest range to the smallest range was 2.67. The World Bank, on the other hand, took a different measure. Instead of measuring the spread of income within each country, they measured the spread of average incomes across all the countries they could assess. The income of the countries at the 90% level was $9500, while the income of the 10% level countries was $800, and the ratio of these numbers is 11.9. It seems to follow that each of the richer countries is relatively egalitarian internally, but there seems to be little pressure towards equality from country to country. Indeed, quite a number of investments in manufacturing facilities are made in relatively low wage countries purely or largely because of this disparity in income levels.

It is important to insert a cautionary remark at this point. It would be easy to jump to the conclusion that the income ratio between countries of

11.9 was inherently evil and that "something should be done about it", and in particular that companies should not take advantage of this difference by relocating a plant from a wealthy to a poor country. Please recall that such a plant relocation will bring new wealth to the poor country, and will remove wealth from the wealthy country. Such a relocation, in fact, is likely to make a modest contribution to the task of reducing the 11.9 ratio to some lower value. We will return to this topic in chapter eleven when we deal with compensating the losers of certain capital market transactions.

[6]   It is acceptable to be rich, as long as you do not become obsessed with the wealth and fall into the trap of worshiping richness. There is quite a long way to travel in getting this idea adopted. It would not be hard to get many people in the finance field to accept the general point. Each of them might be able quickly to think of a colleague who has fallen into this trap in a very obvious fashion. It is very much harder to identify anyone who feels that there is the remotest chance that he might have so fallen himself. "I am still driving last year's Ferrari" will tend to be their response to any personal challenges.

At least some of the traders in the capital markets are obsessed, not with becoming rich, but with "winning" the trading battle. The extent to which they get rich is not the principal objective, it is simply a signal, or a scoring system, which tells them how well they did compared to some of the others. If I earned $20 million last year and you earned $35 million, then I must treat you with considerable respect and I will study your methods, if I can, to learn how you did it. This way I might become a better trader. The fact that neither of us has any real use for the last ten million of our earnings is not the point. The scoring system says we are both winners, but you are more of a winner than I am, and I must respect that. Is this line of thinking an example of being "obsessed with wealth"? It is in a way, but not really in the way the religions were objecting to. Nonetheless, these massive remuneration packages do exert performance pressure on the entities which pay them, and therefore adds to the general transmission of pressure round the entire financial system, as discussed in chapter one, and as shown in diagram two in that chapter.

[9]   The obligation to support the clergy. In the medieval period, making funds available to the clergy was seen as basic insurance for the soul. Any sensible slave trader would build a few churches, or even a cathedral, to persuade the clergy, and therefore perhaps God, to be on his

side. There is clear evidence of this on the Swedish island of Gotland, where the eleventh century pirates built a spectacular collection of churches in Visby, the very beautiful old capital. Some of the elegant public schools in Britain, dating from the nineteenth century but financed from fortunes created earlier, have thought it best not to publicise the source of their original endowments.

The obligation to give resources to the church was first articulated, in each of the four religions we have looked at, by the clergy who would either be the direct beneficiaries or would gain in power by exercising control of the onward transmission of the funds. The public, especially the richer members of the public, who are expected to fulfil this obligation, have become less willing to believe that the duty to donate exists. They note that the tasks formerly performed by the clergy have been increasingly nationalised and secularised. They note that the taxes levied to enable the government to deliver these "social services" appear to them to be getting larger. Some of the taxes actually have become larger. The tendency of some of the clergy to emphasise the "camel and the eye of the needle" when speaking to better off members has also had a cumulatively disenchanting effect.

[10]   The obligation to support the community. This is probably the most important of the unsolved problems of the financial sector. There is a very large number of communities, and if you support one of them you may be damaging another one. If you support your employment community (the financial company or bank you work for) and support your client community (the company which hired your bank) by financing a project to move a factory from the community which is a city in America to the community which is a town in South Africa, you have supported three communities and damaged a fourth. Conflicts like this are impossible to avoid in today's markets.

The typical large business is operating in thirty, forty, or even a hundred countries, and the managers of the business do not normally regard countries as communities. They regard groups of countries as communities. Europe is a community, NAFTA is a community, Asean is a community. When Toyota decided on December 9 1997 to build a car factory in France instead of in Britain, the real decision was the decision to build in Europe; the choice of Britain or France would be a matter of detail, based on such matters as security and balance of risk.   It is very difficult indeed for a finance professional to address the question of community support at a level that is as small as the nation state.

[11]   The concept of interest.   This has been discussed in the previous chapter.   The Islamic concern with the stress which interest can cause is very clearly a valid concern if the doubling and redoubling was really happening.   Even in the Christian world, when interest is compounding, the total liability can become very serious.   In the modern era, however, at least in western countries, the concept of limited liability has become very widespread.   If the liability to pay interest becomes too great, the debtor can seek court protection, or can simply declare himself bankrupt. This means he loses the capital he has put into the venture, but the problem, which was very real in 600 AD, of being sold into slavery, is no longer with us.   Lloyds Insurance market, which was the last major bastion of unlimited liability within the financial sector, has recently been forced to admit that this is no longer a feasible solution, and has admitted "names" on a limited liability basis with effect from 1996.

The problem of interest has changed enormously, but it remains a very serious problem.   The capital structure of a venture ought to be a very specific function of the nature of the venture.   Some of the disastrous investments advocated by the IMF (such as the Tanzanian shoe factory) failed seriously in this regard.   The IMF staff who advocated and then created these projects were theoreticians who had no understanding of business, or marketing, or of financial reality.   These projects were structured with very heavy debt, completely out of line with the business risk structure of the ventures. Several third world countries have been pushed into a state very like slavery because of these projects, which owed more to the need for bureaucrats to fill their quotas of projects than to meaningful economic development.   The World Bank and the IMF are still struggling with these problems, and continue to refuse to admit that they caused the problem in the first place.

[13]   The problem of duty and the problem of obligation to give aid. The Christians have followed the thinking of Mo Ti in promoting the concept of universal love [Jochim 1980].   A person in need should be assisted because of the need, and this obligation to assist is nothing to do with the relationship which might pre-exist between the helper and the aided party.   The Buddhists, always apparently given to positive thinking, have suggested that the person who has an opportunity to assist a fellow human can expect a reward in this life or the next if he seizes that opportunity.   The Buddhists do not, it would seem, regard the idea of obligation as being applicable in this situation.   It is to be looked upon as an opportunity.   The Jews have followed the more restricted route of

imposing obligation on those who have a prior contract. Those who are not Jews should be helped in very precisely defined ways, which are quite generous but subject to specific limitations. The Moslem approach is intermediate between the Jewish and the Christian. The obligation exists to "feed on a day of hunger a closely related orphan or a poor wretch lying in the dust" [90:13-18], and piety includes the giving of one's substance to "kinsman, orphans, the needy, the traveller, beggars, and to ransom the slave" [2:177]. The duty to aid is apparently unrestricted, but those with a contract are at the front of the queue.

An Approach to Two Ethical Commands for Action

On the assumption that we can take the "easy" items as read, it becomes necessary to consider the more difficult ones and see whether they can be formulated effectively into an ethical command of manageable size which will give sound new guidance to finance practitioners, when taken in conjunction with common knowledge and universally applicable laws and rules of behaviour. In fact, it seems to be necessary to produce two ethical commands. A positive one to deal with hoarding, and a negative one to deal with the general duty of caring and avoidance of greed.

Some of the above list of "tricky items" are to be excluded from the ethical commands. The prohibition of interest, and the requirement to support the clergy, will not be part of the ethical commands, for very different reasons.

It has already been reported that the Islamic prohibition on interest seems out of place in the present day economies. It was understandable in 600AD, when the doubling laws were operating, and the possibility of slavery on default was real. Now, it seems quaint, given the protection of the bankrupt available under most regulations. The savings of the cautious are not brought out and re-invested in the community when interest is prohibited, and the whole community loses in material ways as a result. I do not, therefore, plan to advocate this prohibition. Indeed, it would seem more sensible to invite the Uluma to think this one through again; those with the power to bind and to loosen could benefit their people by doing a spot of loosening on this issue. The prohibition is in the Quran, in several places, however, so it would be a huge step for the Islamic communities to make this change. A suggestion which may help them deal with this problem is given in chapter eleven, in the section on new financial instruments.

The requirement to support the clergy is a regulation which most varieties of clergy have been in agreement about. For an MFP, the topic is individually quite simple but collectively rather difficult. Financial trading is global. Each MFP may be able quickly to identify his or her group of clergy. For the major institutions, however, there are dozens of different sects drawn from at least half a dozen different religions to choose among. There is also the problem that there are many secular agencies, some of them government-linked, which are fulfilling many of the same charitable functions as religions and which are in a position to insist on donations from the financial and corporate sectors. It would also be difficult in most large financial institutions for pressure to be exerted on employees to make donations to their own choice of religion; even if this could be attempted, it would be impossible to verify without severe invasions of employee privacy. The decision to support the clergy must be left to individual people, whether they are attached to the financial sector or not.

That leaves hoarding, international and national wage dispersions, obsession with wealth, community support, and the scope of duty. We will consider hoarding first, and then consider, as a group, income dispersion, wealth, community support, and duty.

An Ethical Command about Hoarding

The very reasonable prohibition on hoarding of food is not required in the advanced economies at the present time. The competition to distribute food is very great, and the people are easily able to obtain as much food as they want at prices they can usually afford, if the welfare system is doing its job as well as it does in most advanced countries. In the poorer countries, notably in parts of Africa and Southeast Asia, the distribution system is seriously deficient. There is not enough food there in the first place, and what there is is not efficiently distributed. Hoarding of food is a problem in these countries.

Hoarding of commodities other than food is much less of a problem than it used to be. The Lome convention has significantly damped the volatility of edible commodity prices; not enough for the producers to like the convention, too much for the consumers to like it, but the approach is working reasonably well. The commodity markets, such as the metal exchanges, are set up with special machinery in place to carry out the hoarding collectively. By purchasing a metal when it is low and selling when it is high, the collectively financed metal inventory companies seek to avoid large price fluctuations. Producing nations, usually relatively poor ones, are protected from seriously low prices, while consuming nations, usually rich ones, are protected when there is a shortage.

Hoarding of money, in the Scrooge sense, does not now happen in any significant way. Anyone with a large fortune will almost certainly have placed the funds in an institution on an interest bearing contract or a profit sharing contract. The funds are therefore recycled in some form, and are deployed for the benefit of the owner and of the affected communities, broadly defined. It is possible that a few people continue to have large amounts of cash hidden under the bed, but this is really rare now.

It seems to be the case therefore that the problem of hoarding is real, but is very specific in form. Hoarding of food was the issue when the religions were being written down, and it still is. It is taking place, however, in a very specific group of communities, the poorest countries and especially the rural areas of those countries.

An ethical command for the financial community might then be drafted in a positive form. *Devise a method of financing the food distribution system in poorer countries so that the people there have the same level of access to food as the rural citizens of more advanced nations.* It has proved very hard to do this. The amounts of money which the African rural poor can pay is so small that the distribution system cannot reach them. When charitably inclined groups from the wealthier nations try to provide distributive help directly, this usually works for a while but is then obstructed by various kinds of gangsterism.

It is encouraging to note that progress has been made on the financial aspects of this difficult matter. There was a meeting in Washington in 1997, and another in New York in June 1998, at which the financing issue was addressed. The problem, specifically, was to link the micro-lenders to the global capital markets. Micro-lenders are schemes under which the "bank" extends a very small amount of credit to people who are very poor. The Grameen Bank in Bangladesh, Opportunity, and Accion International are substantially the largest of these micro-lenders, but there are ten thousand such programmes around the world. Most of these are minute, and do not make a profit. The meeting concluded that these micro-lenders are not yet ready to hook up to the capital markets, but that a certain set of specific actions could be taken which would enable them to come to the capital markets collectively in a year or so. One of these actions would entail the creation of an inspection system, to sort out the well-managed from the merely well-meaning. The target of the New York meeting was to achieve loans to a hundred milion poor familes by the year 2005. This is going to be difficult, but it is encouraging that more than a thousand financial institutions from a hundred countries came to the meeting to try to work out how to do it. Once the loan system is in place, the food distribution system will certainly be improved. Indeed, Monsanto is already involved with Grameen in an announced plan for an agricultural advisory scheme in Bangladesh, which has the mission of making that country self-sufficient in maize, rice, and cotton. [Financial Times June 29 1998 Page 3]

The first ethical command is therefore being addressed. We are at an early, perhaps even embryonic, stage in solving the problem, but a lot of people are giving a lot of thought to the task. It is true that the financial community has not so far responded to this ethical command from the religions. However, the financial community is responding now, and no further discussion of this first ethical command will be offered in this book.

An Ethical Command against Financing Deprivation

Four points have been made above. First, that there is a substantial disparity of incomes between countries, and a lesser disparity within them. Second, that the religions are unanimous about the dangers of becoming obsessed with wealth. Thirdly, the religions order us to feel a general obligation to help those who are in trouble and are in need; they differ on the details and the extent of the obligation, but agree that the obligation is real and widely applicable. Fourth, there is a duty to support the community, or society, in which we live and work. The issue now is to work out what this implies for the MFP, either individually, collectively, or corporately.

In part one, the pressures of MFP living were described. There is a continuing search for revenue, and a never-ending obligation to transact so as to create that revenue stream. The decision to purchase or to sell a particular financial instrument is not the subject of very much profound soul-searching about the underlying consequences of the transaction which this instrument will put into operation. The decision is made on the basis of a much simpler question:- "Will it go up in price, or down?" For a second-hand security, that is probably enough. The second hand share market is providing a useful service to holders of small to moderate parcels of shares by enabling them to exit from an investment before the company is wound up, or the project ends by other means. The market also allows the big institutional traders to adjust their portfolios of large holdings quickly and efficiently.   For new securities, and for majority holdings in companies, however, this view is morally insufficient. In both instances, there is a need for the MFP to consider what it is they are doing, and what the moral consequences of the actions they can take might be.

In the case of a new security, the entrepreneurial group will engage a stockbroker or a merchant bank to put the shares on the market. A prospectus will be prepared which states what the business is about, who the present owners are, how many shares are for sale, what the new money will be used for, and what they think the financial results will be for the next year or two.   There is nothing to prevent a discussion of the impact of the new funds on the communities in which the business is situated, but I have never seen any such discussion.   Sometimes there is a comment about enhanced shareholder value through expenditure economies, which is a standard code for laying off people and shutting down facilities, but the affected communities are not discussed.

In the case of a merger, acquisition, or takeover, which are just different words for the same event, there are usually two merchant banks, one helping the bidder and the other helping the managers of the company being bid for. Whether the bid is contested or not, there is a probability that one of the goals of the proposed merger will be cost reduction, which may mean plant closures, personnel layoffs, consolidating movements of a factory in one town into space in another factory in another town, country, or continent. As a general rule, the affected communities have no say in the outcome of these negotiations. There is a good reason for this. The companies probably do not know which communities are going to be affected at the time of the merger. They may not even know if there are going to be any closures or layoffs.   It does no good at all to start rumours of such events, because the existence of the rumour makes the reality much more likely, because of the decline in morale which the rumours cause.

It would be silly to suggest that the financiers involved should regard it as a moral duty never to close a factory. There are many products which come to the end of their lives, and nobody will buy them. The factory which made them will either have to be turned to another task, or closed.

If there are no other tasks available, closure may be the only choice. Closing it quickly may be rather more of a shock than letting it wither, but it is easier to put the workforce into something new if they have been in the habit of producing rather than in the habit of spinning things out.

The normal behaviour of the MFP in these situations is to seek to maximise the realised profits of the institution they are working for. This may mean buying the new shares, or it may mean not buying them, it may mean selling the shares bid for, or it may mean not selling them. Given the four points from the religions, the purely economic basis for the trading decision is simply not enough. We must add something. Something that will not intrude to a damaging degree upon the effectiveness and efficiency of the capital markets, but will make sure, as best anyone can, that the communities prosper, that income dispersions are either reduced or at least not widened, that the injured are given help, and that we ourselves do not become so cash-orientated that the word "obsessed" is applicable.

It is suggested that the modern financial person should think through each major financing project, other than a second hand share trade, with the following maxim in mind, in addition to the usual concerns with profitability and security. The remainder of the book develops this maxim by testing it on a series of typical transactions, and by considering a range of approaches (I have called them "tools") to getting the ethical command adopted.

I do not have the right to finance a transaction which will remove, from anyone, the probability of making a living, without simultaneously procuring the financing of adequate compensation.

It is important to discuss the phrasing of this ethical command. It is written in a manner which will still permit the financial system to function at its customary speed or very near it, but it is intended to make the system function in a very much more humane fashion than it does (sometimes) at the moment.

First, it is a personal ethical command. *I do not have.....* The command may be adopted by a company, and revised accordingly, but for the moment it is a personal belief statement.

The ethical command describes something called the *"probability of making a living"* which definitely needs to be explained. It is important to note that the ethical command does not stop me from financing a transaction that deprives someone of a particular job, nor that deprives a large group from the particular jobs they are now in. It does not commit the MFP to finding the laid-off worker another job. It commits the MFP to investigating what the state of the local job market is, and assessing the probability that the laid-off personnel will get another job. If the local rate of unemployment is 4%, the probability is rather good. If it is 40%, it is very poor. If it is 40% in the local community but 5% in the next-door community, the probability becomes quite good again, but entails moving or commuting costs which have to be compensated for a period.

The ethical command requires the MFP who has examined the situation and concluded that the transaction will, in fact, deprive someone of the *"probability of making a living"* to take some corrective action. The MFP has to *"procure the financing of adequate compensation"*. He does not necessarily have to finance the compensation directly, if there is already a sufficient insurance policy, or government scheme, or other source in operation. He does, however, have to make sure that the other scheme is activated, and that the compensation it provides is actually obtained.

The question of what *"adequate"* means in this context is always going to be judgmental and difficult. This is one of the reasons why even quite well meaning people try to avoid the whole subject.   It is obvious enough to say that compensation is going to lie somewhere between continuing at full salary until the normal retirement age and paying the legal minimum redundancy fee. One large French conglomerate company which faces this situation quite frequently has been paying employees their full rate of base pay (excluding overtime) for a month for every percentage point of unemployment in the town the factory was in, up to a maximum limit. The legal redundancy payment is a part of this total.   The man in the four percent county would get base pay for four months, while the man in the forty percent county would be paid for the company's thirty month maximum.

Does the ethical command deal with the instructions of religion?   It seems to me that it forces the financier to think through the situation quite thoroughly. There is the Good Samaritan caring requirement, looking after the people who have been hurt. The person who procures these payments is clearly placing community ahead of wealth, and may thus claim not to be obsessed by it.

The ethical command does not address the problem of the international inequalities in wage rates. However, it has already been pointed out in an earlier chapter that the basic economic reasons for many financing activities may alleviate the international pay disparities. Moving a business from country A to country B will tend to increase the GNP of B and reduce the GNP of A. Very slightly, perhaps, but the direction of change is clear. If A was a rich country to start with, and B was poor, they will be slightly closer after the move than before it.

It is important to note that the financier would be required by the ethical command to consider the problems of suppliers and customers as well as employees in approach his financing decisions. It would be necessary to apply the ethical command to a supplier, to see if they had alternative customers, if they had other work, if the town was prosperous so that they could find more work, and to ask similar questions. It is, of course, perfectly possible that the financier would conclude that there was no damage to compensate. A proper report, with specific quantifications of the estimates which underly the conclusion, would be a convincing defence against any moralists' questioning.

It should be noted that the company for which the financier is working may decide totally to ignore the ethical command. It, and anyone, can always ignore ethical comands, maxims, and mottoes. If the company did not have the option of making an ethical choice, that situation would be wrong also. In the next part of the book we will examine the second ethical command in operation. Using three case studies and a variety of implementation tools, we will "pre-test" the maxim to see if it helps. Maybe, after that, more companies, more banks, and more MFPs will adopt it instead of ignoring it.

Part Three - Testing, then Marketing, the Ethical Command

Chapter Ten:- Some Financial Transactions for Testing

At this stage in the book we have defined the problem, at first in general terms and then more precisely. In addition we have gone through the religions and tried to extract a list of ethical commands which ought to be obeyed by those working in the capital markets, and which are not being generally or even widely obeyed at present. It is not asserted that these commands are the only ones which could improve the situation. It is, however, forcefully asserted that the financial markets would be doing a better job of the task at hand if they did follow them. Rather to my surprise, it seems to have been possible to boil down the religions' commands to two, and further that one of these is very precise and specialised in the field of food distribution. The decision to leave that one out of this book is not to suggest for a moment that it is unimportant, but rests instead on the fact that it is being worked on at the time of writing by a substantial number of senior financial people:- the problem is recognized and is being addressed. Our present business is to address the issues in the immediate surroundings of the capital markets which are not being addressed as yet, and that is what will be attempted in this closing part of the book.

Our task in this part is to take a list of six of the possible steps we could take to improve the moral performance of the capital markets, and a selection of three reasonably typical capital market activities, and the second ethical command of the religions, and work through them systematically. The purpose of this working is not to eliminate any of the combinations from future consideration, but to work out, on a balance of probabilities, which approach has the best chance of making an early difference to practice.

In the present chapter, we will look at the three capital market activities from a conventional financial and economic point of view. This chapter can safely be skipped over by those who are familiar with financial operations. It is included to assist those who are not familiar with a plant relocation financing project, a merger financing, or with a stock option. No attempt is made in this chapter to introduce ethical thinking to the analysis. These are "case studies" which will be used in the tests in the next chapter.

Case Study One:- Plant Relocations

The larger companies have been expanding their horizons with considerable energy in the last twenty years, and they now commonly regard themselves as global enterprises. The head office may be in Tokyo or New York, or London, or Frankfurt, but the operations are managed on a global basis, with the expectation that the product or service will be the outcome of the efforts of managers and staff in several locations, probably situated on at least two different continents.

There are very acute competitive pressures on companies in every industry. These have been touched on earlier in this book. The squeeze between the demands of the shareholding institutions for higher prices and higher profits on the one side, versus the demands of the customers for lower prices and profits on the other, is tightening by the day. The search for a competitive advantage is not an occasional response to a perceived difficulty, but a permanent managerial task, which never stops. One of the ways managers can try to solve the squeeze is to reduce the costs of operations, which allows the prices to be reduced or held (pleasing the customers) while also enabling profits to be increased or held (which pleases the shareholders). One method of cost reduction, in turn, is to take advantage of differences in costs of materials and labour in different countries, or in different districts within a country.

The idea of processing a mined product near the mine is intuitively attractive, in that it saves carrying the unwanted elements any further than is essential. Refining oil near the main fields is desirable for similar reasons. Timber, minerals, oils, rubber, and other natural commodities and products are very much easier to obtain in some countries than in others, and most global corporations are acting on this fact.

The difference in wage rates within a country is typically quite small if the economy is fairly advanced but rather wide when the economy is relatively under-developed. A ratio of from three to eight prevails within each of the OECD countries. The figures for within the developing countries are rather uncertain, but the World Bank has found examples in which the ratio was ten and thirty. When you compare average wage rates between countries, however, the range is much wider. The richest countries have per capita incomes in the region of $10,000, while the poorest countries have incomes of about $200, a ratio of fifty. We previously looked at the inter-decile range, which was a still substantial ratio of just under twelve.

In this context, it is obvious that plant location decisions are potentially useful sources of cost reduction. If a factory in a $10,000 country employing a thousand people can be replaced by a factory in a $1,000 country employing two thousand people, and if the output is just as good after a settling-in period, the global company is eight million a year better off. The people in the poor country are also (usually) better off as well, because the two million they are generating is normally an addition to the previous total. The people who lose, of course, are the thousand in the rich country who are laid off, and, indirectly, the other people in that same rich country who may have to pay for their unemployment benefit.

If the plant relocation project is of the form discussed above, the managers of the global enterprise have several choices to make. Assuming the eight million cost saving actually happens, they can cut the price of the final product by an amount which "gives" the whole amount to the customers, thereby almost certainly inducing a major, and presumably profitable, increase in the total volume of the product sold. Alternatively, they can retain the whole amount, and use the proceeds to pay a higher dividend to the shareholders or to buy back shares from the shareholders. They can, obviously, choose any intermediate course.

The managers of the global enterprise will carry out a very standardised computation in deciding whether to do this plant relocation or not. The computation is called a discounted cash flow analysis, and I am not going to reproduce this analysis here because it is very fully discussed in every introductory finance textbook which has been written since 1955 [Brealey, Myers, and Marcus 1999, for example]. The cash flows (inward and outward) that will arise if you do not move the plant are estimated. The cash flows (in and out) that will arise if you do move it are estimated. The initial costs of moving the factory's machinery, the costs of training the new workforce, the costs of paying redundancy to the old workforce, the cost (if any) of cleaning the old site up are estimated, the incentives (if any) offered by the new site government are estimated. Taxation, in both the old and the new site, must be taken into consideration. The time it will take to get the new workforce up to a high enough standard of production is often the hardest single item to be estimated. After all this, the sum can be done, and the economic value of the proposed move is obtained. The project either does, or does not, provide a sufficient return on the capital that it will absorb.

The bankers to the global enterprise will usually take the global enterprise's calculations at their face value if the firm has a reasonably good record of effective management in the past. The banker will therefore be able, quite easily, to say yea or nay to any funding requirement the management want from him. It is unusual for a plant relocation to be so large as to involve an investment bank, but the task is a reasonably simple one if that does come about.

In corporate capital expenditure manuals, detailed instructions are provided for handling various kinds of computation and various kinds of cash flow. The word "ethics" does not normally appear in these manuals. I took the liberty of photocopying one of the exceptions. "If any person from outside the group, and especially any government agent, uses words such as ethical, unethical, moral, or immoral in connection with a project covered by this manual, such an incident must be reported immediately to the group head office legal department"

Case Study Two:- The Corporate Merger or Acquisition

There are numerous reasons why a merger or acquisition or takeover can occur. [1] In the case of a family business, they may simply have nobody left who can run it, or who wants to run it. Selling out makes a good deal of sense in that situation. [2] A small firm may have a really good idea or a really powerful product, but not have the money to get it to market quickly enough to beat larger companies with a similar idea. The small firm may be better to sell itself, for a rather hefty price, into a big one which can move things along more quickly. [3] A defective management group, which nonetheless holds a large block of shares, may have failed to deliver, and the rest of the shareholders may simply be so fed up that they will sell the company as the only way to resolve a very unsatisfactory state of affairs.

Hostile takeovers are much less common, but they usually arise for fairly similar reasons. The shareholders of "A" company are invited to sell their shares to "B" company, and they have to decide whether this is a good thing or not. The shareholders of "A" may be induced to sell by the high price of the "B" shares they are offered. They may be attracted by the apparently superior prospects which seem to lie in the future when the two firms are brought together. They may simply be fed up with the rotten results obtained by the managers of "A", and want to get out while they have the opportunity.

There are some who make careful distinctions between the words, merger, acquisition, and takeover. Unfortunately, these careful distinctions are not all the same as each other, and there is no real agreement on their exact meaning. An acquisition and a takeover are usually taken to be synonyms by almost everyone. A merger is usually meant to imply the coming together of equals. In practice, it usually becomes very obvious that they were not equal at all, and that the smaller of the two firms has actually been consumed by the larger.

In any event, the merger event is a significant one for the capital markets. The fees paid by companies for advice during these episodes are very large. There was a merger being negotiated at the time of writing this chapter, involving GTE, Worldcom, MCI, and BT. The fees which might be received by the lawyers and the merchant banks and the investment banks for this transaction, if it were to be consummated, would be slightly less than a billion dollars. A large part of the fee total was dependent on there being a transaction. If the whole negotiation collapsed, for any reason, the lawyers and bankers do not receive any fee. It is possible that some of them may be influenced towards the achievement of a deal by this feature of the contracts under which they are working. In this particular instance, Worldcom and MCI merged, so a portion of the contingent fees was earned, or at least paid.

When a merger negotiation is happening, the economic issues that have to be handled are as complicated and intricate as any that can arise in private sector work. Usually, the plan is that company "B" will issue its own shares to the shareholders of company "A", in exchange for the shares they held in company "A" before the merger. Sometimes there will be a cash payment in addition, which increases the amount the company "A" holders receive. Occasionally, there will be other instruments offered as part of the exchange price.   There may be bonds, or convertible bonds, or preferred shares, or warrants, or other instruments designed to make the whole deal look more attractive to the shareholders of company "A". Their basic and simple task, from an economic standpoint, is to make sure that they get paid more, preferably significantly more, than the price quoted on the stock exchange for the shares they are giving up.

Historically, the shareholders of the assorted companies "A" have done this rather well. The shareholders of the companies taken over have been been found to obtain a very large proportion of the net benefits of any mergers that have taken place between companies quoted on the major markets since the second world war. [Asquith 1983]

The transactions are normally carried out with a very high level of efficiency and effectiveness. The very highly paid merchant bankers, accountants, and lawyers deliver a spectacular level of instantaneous service, involving extremely detailed transaction contracts which might be agreed in principle at a dinner at 9pm and which are available as fully fledged contracts, perhaps a thousand pages in total length, at 7am the next day. If there turns out to be a dispute on a point, or one of the contracting parties wants to adjust something and manages to get the other party to agree to that change, the revised contracts will be generated in a couple of hours. And, at least in my own limited experience of this, they will be faultless. The merger service machinery is impressive; the reader may fairly comment that they ought to be at the prices they charge, but at least the standard of service is superb.

The computations which have to be performed for the consummation of a merger transaction are far too technical for the scope of this book. The two companies have different earnings histories, different cash flow histories, different dividend payment histories, different asset valuations. There are complex and arcane sums that have to be done to try to work out a reasonable basis upon which they ought to be brought together. Most commonly, the goal is to share the ownership of the combined entity in proportion to the earning power of the two component firms, mediated by the other factors, especially growth rates. However, these sums are just that; they are only sums. The items which are considered by the merchant bankers and the accountants and the lawyers are quantitative measures of the performance of the two businesses, and they do not really measure the essence of the marriage that is proposed.

That essence lies within the minds and hearts and emotions of the people who lead the two firms. That essence also reflects the will, the strength, the minds and hearts and emotions of the people who work under the direction of those leaders. You might call this element in the equation "esprit de corps". Or maybe "morale". Making a merger successful is a much more intricate task than getting agreement that it should take place.

Among the financial institutions who hold the shares in the two companies, and who therefore have more say than anyone else on whether it will happen or not, the decisions on a hostile merger are usually made on a purely financial and economic basis. However, the judgements to be made are not easy, and they are very much to do with morale, and the leadership qualities of the people. Will the "A" management really be able to get their act together and produce the earnings they claim in their defense document? Will the "B" managers really be able to put through the cost savings they claim in their merger proposal document? The esprit de corps and morale issues are very much under consideration while the financial institutions which own the shares are trying to make up their minds.

After the merger has been put through, there is an assumption that the cost savings claimed will be achieved by the successful acquirer. There will be a rationalisation of the facilities. We do not need two head office buildings. In fact, there is a substantial list of things we do not need two of. Therefore there will be a gradual elimination of people, of factories, of service centres, of branches, of vehicles, of sales outlets, and of products and services. After the rationalisation phase, if everything has gone reasonably well, there will be an expansion phase. This will involve an expansion of the number of people employed, factories, vehicles, branches, and so on, but they will be in different places and serving different markets than the ones that have been pared away. Most successful mergers lead to expansion eventually; unfortunately it is not common for the people who were rationalised out at the time of the merger to participate in the eventual expansion.

Case Study Three:- The Option Contract

In 1997, the Nobel Prize for Economics was awarded to Myron Scholes and Robert Merton. Fischer Black and Myron Scholes published their excellent paper on the pricing of options in 1972, building on the work of Robert Merton a couple of years earlier. Sadly, Black died before he knew of the award, which he would otherwise (almost certainly) have deservedly shared with the other two. The difficulties which Scholes and Merton got into in 1998 as partners in Long Term Credit Management of Greenwich were not related to their brilliant conception of the right way to value a tradeable option

A call option is a contract between two people or firms, under which "A" acquires the right, but not the obligation, to purchase, on or before a known future date, a thousand shares in a named company from "B" at a price determined now. In exchange, "A" pays "B" a fee now. A put option is exactly the same, except that it gives "A" the right to sell the share to "B" instead of buying it from him.

We are now dealing with a transaction which lies at the inner heart of the financial markets. There are a few outsiders who dabble in options, and a reasonable number of knowledgeable individuals who trade in options as a principal activity, but by and large options trading is a game for the professionals only. It is a big game. Nearly a quarter of all the transactions based on the common stock (=ordinary shares) of American companies in 1996 were effected through the options market.

The reason for the popularity of options among the professionals in the capital markets is that they allow fund managers to make temporary changes to the portfolio they are managing at very much lower costs than would be incurred if they were to buy or to sell the shares themselves. Suppose we have a portfolio which consists, for simplicity, solely of twenty million shares of General Widgets.   These are selling for five pounds each, so the portfolio stands at a hundred million. As a fund manager, we are quietly proud of ourselves, because it has recently moved up to this level from 350p, and we are confident that the trustees of the fund will renew our contract when the decision has to be taken in a month's time.   At the same time, we are a little bit nervous. There have been a few bits of disturbing gossip about General Widgets, to the effect that the chairman is being investigated for tax complications and is losing his grip. We could, of course, lock in the profit by selling the holding at five pounds, paying a commission on the sale of about one half of one per cent of the fund. That is a lot of money, at half a million. Also, there is a chance that selling twenty million shares would cause the price to fall quite a bit from the five pound price. Instead, we might consider buying a put option on all or part of the holding. Suppose we bought 20,000 put contracts at 475p for £100,000. Each of these contracts would entitle us to sell one thousand shares at the striking price of 475p. The worst that could happen now would be for the shares to fall below 475p, whereupon we would exercise the put. The fund would be sitting on £94.9 millions in cash when the trustees have to vote to renew our contract, which compares quite favourably with the £70 millions the fund was worth when the shares were worth 350p. Of course, if the shares go up instead, we would simply write off the cost of the put, and never exercise it. This is called locking in a profit. The example given is rather a large scale one. Most portfolios consist of many holdings, so each of the option purchases would have been smaller in size.

Another application of the option is to take advantage of an anticipated increase in the value of a share. The traditional way to do this, of course, is to buy the share. You spend a million of the fund's money on buying a hundred thousand shares at ten pounds each, and wait until the price goes up to twelve, when you sell. The more modern way to do the same thing would be to buy a hundred call option contracts at £1,000 each with a striking price equal to the current price of ten pounds. When the share price moves up, it drags the call option price up with it. If the share went from ten to twelve, the call would go from one to three, approximately. This means that the same gain would be obtained through the option route as through the purchase route, but would involve the initial outlay of only £100,000 instead of £1,000,000.

This may appear to be some kind of black magic. It is not. It is a matter of selling the risk in a transaction to someone else. The buyer of an option is transferring risk to the seller of the option, who is known as the "writer". The writer of the put option in the first example is undertaking to buy our General Widgets shares at 475, in the full knowledge that we will not exercise our option if the price is higher than that. His fee for selling the option has been set to reflect his estimate of the price drop happening. Remember that he collects the fee whether the price goes down or not. In the second example, the writer of the call option is undertaking to sell us the share at ten on a future date when the price might have gone up to twelve. His fee for selling the option reflects his estimate of the likelihood of that happening. Most option writers are very large financial institutions, especially large insurance companies. They can take these chances, partly because they are big enough to write a large number of them which they hope will more or less cancel out.

How, if at all, can this rather arcane contract possibly affect ordinary folk? The main problem is that the overall level of risk in the market is increased by the existence of the derivative securities, of which options are the most important example. If the first fund could not trade by buying put options, they would have had to sell the shares to eliminate the possibility of loss. Since they can trade in options, they are willing to take the risk of holding the shares, and letting the insurer guarantee their risk by taking on the mirror image of that risk. The insurance company is, to that extent, less safe as a repository of the ordinary citizen's cash than it would have been if had not been writing options. There is no real check on their allegation that the options they write cancel out.

In the next chapter, we will use these typical, routine, corporate finance transactions as case studies. The main objective is to explore a range of methods or approaches or tools which may make it easier for finance people to avoid unethical financing actions. As each tool is considered, we will be using the three case studies to test it for ethical effectiveness.

Chapter Eleven:- Political and Organisational Tools for Gaining
Acceptance for an Ethical Command

In this chapter we will look at a list of the tools which might be used to
try to achieve higher ethical standards within the financial sector. Each
tool is a political, theological, or organisational approach to achieving
change in the way financings are done. For each tool, we will first
discuss its general nature, and how it might be put into operation. After
that we will look at how the tool might be employed to adjust one or
more of the three investment projects which were examined
economically in chapter ten. The goal of this study will be to see
whether the tool will help fulfil the second ethical command, the one
about deprivation of a probability of earning a livelihood, or whether it
will hinder. The first ethical command, about food distribution
financing, will only be touched upon lightly in this part of the book.

The three investment projects are the plant location decision, the merger,
and the traded option sale. The six tools, which are arranged in an
increasing order of human compulsion, are prayer, mind expansion and
training, a new reward system for financial service employees, an ethical
impact report, a new capital instrument, and legal compulsion and
prohibition. These solutions are independent of one another, so they
could, perhaps slightly improbably, all be used at once.

Prayer

There are many kinds of prayer in use in the major theistic religions.
Prayers of adoration, prayers of confession, and prayers of gratitude are
offered up all over the world. Some of these are answered, some are not.

In the context of this project, the most important kind of prayer would be
a prayer of intercession. The believers ask God to take action to bring
about some change in the world that the believer wants, either for himself
or for someone else he regards highly. "Give wisdom to our
government". "Strengthen our army as it faces the enemy". "Help Aunt
Jane get over her influenza". "Give me strength to fight against the bad
proposal that will affect my fellow-employees and me at work". As
with other prayers, the response of God is variable, ranging from
instantaneous granting of the plea to ignoring it completely.

There are, however, at least three other things that happen when a supplication is made publicly, whether during a worship service or otherwise. First, the praying person exposes his wish to other people. Second, the congregation may choose to add their own voices to that of the original supplicant. Third, it is possible that the idea may spread from one place of worship to others nearby, and perhaps eventually across an entire denomination or even to other denominations. It is clear that there are only certain kinds of topic which have the potential to spread in this fashion. It is conceivable that our business in this book may have that potential. It will need to be packaged carefully if that is to happen.

The positive instructions from the religions about food distribution are relatively easy to formulate in a prayer. "Please help our financiers to work out ways of helping the farmers and food processing companies to get food to the poorest parts of the poorest nations on a consistent basis".

If the financiers want some assistance in working out ways in which this could be done on a profit-making basis, which is the only way it can be done so that it will last, the ideas underlying the Grameen Bank might be worth looking at. [Holcombe, 1995, esp Ch 3]

On the negative command, about livelihoods and compensation, the following text might be offered as a first draft. We will try to produce something a bit less lumbering in the next paragraph. "Please force our bankers and investment houses to understand that they do not have the right to finance a transaction which will obliterate the probability of earning a livelihood of any person, unless they also procure the financing of full compensation for that deprivation". It certainly doesn't exactly trip off the tongue, as phrased above. It says what we mean, and God will understand it, but quite a few of the preachers and the congregations will not have a clue what we are on about.

How about this, then. "Please help the financiers and business leaders to look beyond the economics of their decisions so that they may be aware of the people their decisions will damage, and so that they will realise they have no right to cause such damage without also financing compensation". Better, I think. Perhaps good enough, if there are backup materials available so that the financial people can find out what we mean in some detail, and so that the congregations can be sufficiently clearly informed about what they are being asked to endorse. There are some such materials already, of course. Sadly, they tend to be written in a regrettably hysterical tone, which just does not get any attention at all in financial circles.

If the churches get together and offer this prayer up, or some reasonably close variant of it, and the congregations start asking these questions of the bankers they run into, and the story starts to get backing from the politicians and the papers and the television stations, who are all pretty good at spotting a bandwagon, we might just get somewhere.

The impact of prayer on the achievement of the two commands is not only hard to predict, it is, for the believer, presumptuous to make the attempt. In the setting of the traded option, the consequence of a prayer cannot be predicted at all. In the settings of a plant location or of a merger, the consequence might be humaneness on the part of one of those who have power to act, or toughness on the part of those in government roles, who can impose conditions before allowing the transaction to happen.

Mind expansion and Training

The next tool or solution would involve educating all the people who work in the financial industry on the nature of financial ethics so that they will be able to work out what actions would be ethical more easily than before. This solution cannot be expected to operate quickly, but it may be the surest route in the longer term.

This solution is founded on the belief that the people who work in the financial markets are not in any sense unethical by choice. The problem is that they are situated in a job which has reasonably clear cut rules. They have been instructed that certain kinds of actions will be rewarded and certain other actions will be penalised. The more senior among them have been told that certain kinds of judgements must be made, and if they do a good job of this (=make a profit) they will be rewarded, while if they make a poor job of it (=guess what) they will not have much chance of promotion. It is not seen, by anyone, as an ethical question. It is a cash question. We put in a pound, and we got out L1.25, so all must be well.

The decision appears to be freed of its ethical content by the distance which exists between the financial investor or his agent and the physical actions which may have an ethical impact. The investor sends money to a financial management company. The management company buys a share in a quoted corporation. The corporation allocates some of the money to one of its subsidiaries, located in any one of the world's two hundred countries. The subsidiary decides to shut down a plant in another country, at a location of serious unemployment within a nation of little natural wealth. There is a long organisational distance between the investor and the employees of the closed plant. It is not realistic to expect the ultimate investor to be able to prevent unethical actions at this organisational range. The ethical thinking must be done at a point closer to the unethical action.

In the specific situation discussed in the previous paragraph, the correct place for ethical thinking to occur would be at the top of the subsidiary that is closing the plant. That officer should make restitution to the eliminated employees. If that officer does not, the top brass of the corporation should insist on restitution being made. If they do not, the investors should take action. There is a very real problem here, in that the investors may simply not know what has happened.

This is really no different from the reality in other aspects of corporate life. The investor does not really know what is going on, in any detail, in the dozens of subsidiaries owned by a company in which he holds shares. This is true of product launches, of factory openings and closings, and of a thousand other activities which happen every day. The shareholder does not know the details except insofar as the managers tell him about it, or, in more extreme cases, if the auditor decides it needs to be reported on. The routine reports of companies are really quite informative, but they are limited in what they can convey. As a general rule, the law specifies what must be included and what general form the report must take on. In addition to the law, the institutes of chartered accountants or certified public accountants periodically decide that a new item ought to be reported on. These institutes have so far been reluctant to get into the business of reporting on ethical matters, on the understandable grounds that they are seen as matters of opinion, and that there is quite enough trouble trying to work out what the profit was.

There would appear to be an impasse. The auditors will not inform the investor about an ethical violation. The company may well not inform the investor either. The law does not require anyone to inform the investor about an ethical violation unless is happens to be against the law as well, and there are many instances when the law does not require the investor to be informed then either. Newspapers might try to create a fuss locally, but it is not very likely that the newspapers in the corporation's home country will pick the topic up unless they are desperately short of news.

We cannot expect to get past this impasse at the beginning of the financial ethics programme. We will have to start on a smaller scale, within the home nation of the corporation. We can go multinational later. Within the home nation, we have a slightly easier task. The auditors still will do nothing, as will the corporation. The law will similarly evade the issue, because there is no tort for suit if the redundancy minima have been paid. That means we have to rely on the media. A number of specific cases will have to be brought forward and exposed, where an investor or an investment company has financed a transaction which deprived one or more persons from the probability of a livelihood within the investment company's home country, and preferably in a case where that country is the corporation's home country too. The objective must be to increase the pressure, and gradually to get an acceptance among the people at large that you should not deprive people of the probability of a livelihood. Not without compensation, at least.

Concurrently, there is a need for training programmes which assist people who are about to enter the financial sector to understand and think about the ethical consequences of what they are doing. There will be many who do not want to listen to such a message, and there will be others who listen at the time but who forget it all under the pressures of the work environment. But some will remember, and act accordingly. I have now taught the first offering of a course called "Financial Ethics" to the honours year BCom students at Edinburgh University, between January and April 1998. They seem to have absorbed some of the ideas, including the one about livelihood deprivation, with enthusiasm. They seem to have listened to some of the other ideas on financial ethics, notably the golden rule, with reservations. The second offering, to the class of 1999, elicited a different reaction. They seem to have adopted a rather Aristotelean line, where the negative command is a particular case of virtue. We will see what happens next year.

In the case of the first two of our worked examples, the plant relocation and the merger, it would be desirable if the result of the mind expansion and training programme could be to cause the financier to think through the consequences of the financing. This would require him to take note of the relocation and to take steps to see about employment rates in the relevant communities and regions. In the case of the merger it would require the analysis of the claimed savings, to find out exactly which duplications were to be eliminated, and to verify that some provident arrangements for the people were in place. As already mentioned, there are several forms this provision could take, and it is perfectly possible that no further funding is needed. However, if the results of these investigations were to be unsatisfactory, the financier would have an obligation to make direct arrangements for improving the situation, at the expense of the client company. The financier is in a position to compel ethical behaviour on the part of the company, on pain of refusal of the capital injection.

It is very important that general opinion among financiers should move away from the current state, which is essentially to claim that the actions of the companies in which they invest are nothing to do with the financier at all. The opinion should move towards a new state, in which the financing of an unethical action is seen as itself unethical. The main responsibility should remain with the person who does the unethical action directly, but the person who financed it is an accomplice.

The arguments of Milton Friedman are perhaps at their most dangerous in the context of this tool or solution. His basic view was set out in the chapter he shared with Steven Kerr. The job of the business executive, says Friedman, is to get as much profit for his shareholders, including himself if applicable, as he can possibly accumulate by legal means. It is for others to fuss about distributions afterwards. It is obvious, if we were considering using the legal tool to bring the ethical command to fruition, that that is exactly what would occur. The legal system (which obviously includes the taxation and social security systems) would take some money from the shareholders and give a fraction of it to those whose probability of earning a livelihood had been impaired, if they happen to reside in the same jurisdiction.

The legal approach has several deficiencies, and these in turn bring out the deficiencies in Friedman's argument. First and second, the amounts taken from the shareholders and given to the redundant will both be the subject of prolonged, perhaps permanent, disputation. Some will say that one is too high and the other too low, and some will say it is the other way around. The legal system is a recipe for continuing discontent. More importantly, thirdly, the legal/tax/social security approach lets all the financiers and all the business people off the hook. They may argue, legitimately, that "I do not have to think about the redundant, that is a task for the government". Having mentally divested the responsibility, the manager can simply quote Friedman and ignore the damage he has done and feel totally justified in doing so. So can the financier who made the transaction possible. Fourthly, and most important of all, the speed with which the damage can be done and the speed with which the law can respond are hopelessly different. The manager can close a plant in a couple of days, given that he has a few years of rotten results from it. It will take the best of governments only a few days to activate the dole system, but months or years to get any positive remedies into play.

The mind expansion approach works by asking the executives to think it through in advance, and to work out alleviating actions in advance, and to develop outplacement counselling schemes in advance or at least concurrently. The best employers already do this, or some of it. It is very important to get the responsibility for doing these things embedded in the minds of all the executives and especially in the minds of all the financiers, who see a dozen of these transactions for every one that a business executive sees. That way, the unavoidable redundancy is not compounded by an avoidable trauma.

We have now considered two of the possible tools, and the diagram below is a summary of the results so far. We will gradually build up this diagram as we work forward through the six tools. The top row of boxes are the column headings, and these show that the remaining rows indicate the nature of the tool, how it performed on the three tests of plant location, merger, and option, and gives an opinion on whether the tool shows promise or should be dropped.

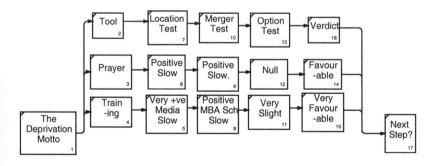

While both prayer and training are being designated as promising tools for the implementation of the ethical motto, both are admitted to be likely to be rather slow in operation, and the training route is likely to require a boost from the news media and from the business schools if it is to make any serious headway. We have made a certain amount of progress with our first two tools, let us now press forward and consider tools three and four.

Changes to the Finance Industry's Reward System

In this section of the chapter, we will take a look at the possibility that we might improve our ethical score in the financial sector by using the payments system tool.

We earlier considered Steven King's paper on reward systems. The futility of rewarding people for doing one thing and then expecting them to do something different from that one thing was made clear. In the financial services industry, there is a strong emphasis on payment by results. A trader who makes a profit expects to get a sizeable chunk of that profit. A trader who makes a loss is less keen on the idea of taking his share of that, but quite a few firms operate on that basis, deducting loss commissions from the next available gains. Other firms pay their front line personnel on the basis of a salary and a bonus, where the bonus is a large proportion of the total, and where the bonus reflects the overall profitability of the trader, or of the small team of which he is a part, or (less commonly, I believe) of the entire firm.

This means that the trader is powerfully motivated towards thinking that a transaction, whatever its consequences, is very likely to be better than no transaction. Further, a profitable transaction is virtually certain to be better than an unprofitable one. With an unprofitable transaction, you can at least get some credit for having tried.

Those employed in the financial industries in non-trading tasks are also orientated towards action. A client who manages to escape from his bank branch without having been sold something is, nowadays, showing significant determination. A dozen years ago, banks did not have any sales staff; the bank manager was responsible for the customer interface, which involved making sure that the bank was available when a client wanted to borrow something, but it was not considered proper to speak of selling. Now, about an eighth of all the staff in the retail banks have the selling duty specifically in their job specification and a further eighth are completely allocated to this role. There is a difference here between the retail bankers and the traders discussed above, in that the bankers are not paid, normally, on a straight commission basis. At the same time, a bank employee who has a sales responsibility knows that he or she has to earn a certain number of points during the month. You get X points for selling a life policy, and Y points for selling a loan, and Z points for selling a mortgage, and so on. As long as X+Y+Z is greater than the target, you remain in work.

The recent fuss about the mis-selling of personal pensions is a classic illustration of Mr Kerr's principle at work. The independent financial advisors were offered generous commissions by the various pension providing insurers for selling these policies. Senior managers within the providers had targets which they were expected to attain, in terms of the number and value of the personal pension contracts they were to procure through the independent financial advisors. The providers expected the IFA to avoid selling to those for whom the personal pension would not be appropriate, and the more cautious of them built in a safeguard in the form of a department which checked the attributes of the personal pension against those of the company scheme the client was thinking of leaving. Most of these more cautious houses came away from the episode without serious difficulty, but many of the providers who relied on the IFAs to carry out the value check are in deep trouble now. If you pay someone for action, and do not pay him for inaction, you will get action.

It is simple and easy to say that the solution might be to change the way in which the employees of financial institutions are rewarded. It is very much more difficult to do. If an investment bank were to put its traders on a flat salary, without a performance bonus, it is, I believe, safe to predict that they would lose all their trading staff within a month. Unless, of course, the flat salary was extremely high, in which case the employees would remain but would not do very much. A major investing house that was going to move over to a buy-and-hold strategy from an active trading strategy might be able to do this. There are very few of those.

There can be no doubt that the aggressive tactics of Goldman Sachs and Salomon has paid off for them, and there can be no doubt either that they have a reward structure which is as results-linked as you could possibly get. The British retail banks are also, in their very different way, moving towards a results-linked management style. In fact, I can think of no significant group of financially orientated companies which are moving away from a results-linked style and towards a community-role style. The traffic is all in the other direction.

At first sight, this looks a rather worrying conclusion. How on earth are we going to get the financial institutions to pay attention to the ethical command if they are putting more and more pressure on themselves to generate results, with the inevitable corner-cutting which that is likely to bring about? I suggest that we will be able to rely on the very strong preference of financial institutions for being governed by self-regulation. They do not readily accept orders from government, and when they think one is about to come along they will try very hard to get their own trade association to pass a regulation that will enable the same result to be achieved but with less law, less officialdom, less bureaucracy, and probably less expense.

Perhaps the goal can be achieved by waiting until there is a clear case of violation of the ethical command. A financial institution underwrites a venture which will have the clear consequences of throwing a substantial number of people out of work in a location where there are no other employers, in circumstances in which it is clear that neither the corporation nor the institution are inclined to compensate adequately. A joint effort, involving a couple of newspapers, a couple of TV stations, an opposition MP who both believes in the concept and wants some publicity, and perhaps a union if there is one involved, can be mounted to suggest that a change in the compensation law is required. This may have any one of three results. The ethical command becomes law. The ethical command is prevented from becoming law by becoming a "statement of best practice" by the relevant professional association. Or nothing happens at all, in which case we have to wait for another, more blatant, example, and try again.

If, against all the odds, the reward system within the financial sector <u>were</u> to be changed, we can assume that Kerr's law will remain in force. The employees will do what the pay system pushes them towards, ninety-nine times per hundred. At present, agreeing a financing for a plant relocation is a moderately rewarding action for the bank and it would be common for a commission to be paid to the employee(s) who made it happen. The same is true for making an option trade. Arranging the financing for a merger is the merchant banker's equivalent of winning the lottery, except that the merger financing pays more.

If an institution were to introduce a flat salary reward system, and if this were set at a high enough level to avert a mass exodus, the employees could be expected to become less action orientated. It could be assumed that mergers would contine to be financed, but less often and only at the instigation of the would-be predator company, not (usually) at the instigation of the merchant bank. Plant relocations are already instigated, in the main, by the companies, and would probably continue at about the same level. If the bank was expected to implement the ethical command on financing compensation for loss of the probability of a livelihood, it would probably charge a fee for doing so, which might very slightly diminish the demand for such deals.

The trade in options would continue in very much the same way as before. These are now commodity priced products, which are definitely profitable to the banks, but which are also very well appreciated by customer companies. There is a good economic reason to go on buying them, and the writers have a good economic reason to go on selling them in numbers limited by the risk bearing capacity of the insurance company which wrote the option. We are not yet at a level where major insurers are at risk. There are small ones who may appear to be pushing their luck, but only a very few.

In short, if we could wave a magic wand and switch everyone in the financial sector from commission to salary overnight, then I seriously suggest that almost nothing would happen that is different from what is already happening now. The addition of the requirement to fulfil the ethical command on livelihoods would be easier to introduce under such a new reward system, but very little else would change. However, as I made clear at the beginning of this section, I really do not know how any such change as this could be put into operation.

It is possible, I suppose, that one very highly respected chairman of one very large bank might simply go ahead and order the change. If his bank then went on to make the same or more profits from a holding strategy than the others were making from frantic trading the alteration might become more widespread. I do not, however, regard this move as imminent.

Ethical Impact Reports

This fourth tool or approach to the implementation of the ethical command on financial ethics would involve the production of an ethical impact report as part of the documentation of a new financial transaction.

	Location 1 Yanblu	Location 2 Glasgow	Location3
New Livelihoods			
a] New Hires direct	2700		
b] Hires by new suppliers	425		
c] New Outlet hires	225		
Changed Livelihoods			
a] Direct switches		275	
b] Supplier switches		125	
c] Outlet switches		50	
Terminated Livelihoods			
a] Direct terminations		1850	
b] Supplier terminations		380	
c] Outlet layoffs		177	

Preliminary format of the Ethical Impact Report, part one, showing the number of livelihoods affected by the proposed plant relocations. All entries in italics are intended to simulate the handwritten entries arising in a particular plant relocation proposal. These numbers are completely fictitious.

A bank, or merchant bank, or investment bank, which wanted to establish that ethical considerations were being taken into account while investments were being evaluated would specify that an ethical impact report be included in the documentation. The questions to be included in the form would seek to establish whether the ethical command, which was derived from the religions earlier, was being observed.

Once it is established that there will be some kind of livelihood impact of the financing under consideration, it is obligatory to follow up an analysis of the following kind. I have prepared a form, not because that is essential to the task, but because it is the easiest way to put this kind of thinking into operation. The form, with some illustrative numbers which are totally fictional, is shown on the previous page. This identifies, for every affected location, the number of livelihoods affected. The table shows, firstly, all the completely new livelihoods which the financing being planned will bring into existence. This is divided into [1] hires of new employees, [2] contracts anticipated with new suppliers and the headcount effect on those suppliers, and [3] contracts anticipated with new outlets other than company-owned outlets, giving the headcount effect on them. The second section deals with livelihoods which are changed by the project being financed. This would arise if a job, for instance, were converted from being a task for an employee into being a task for a supplier. It could also arise if a task formerly done by an outside contractor were to be taken in-house. If an automation project entailed a substantial layoff of manual workers, and some of these workers were to be retrained to operate the new machinery, this transition would appear under this heading. The last section would deal with livelihoods that were to be terminated as a result of the project being financed. As in the other sections, this would differentiate between employees, suppliers, and outlets.

The questions which have to be asked next are almost self-evident in the light of the earlier discussion in this book. The figures in the illustration show that the company has closed a plant in Glasgow and opened a plant in Yanblu, Sumatra. In the process, nearly 2000 workers at the Glasgow plant are re-assigned or terminated. Some supplier companies also lose contracts and some outlets are closed. These items are routine consequences of a plant relocation exercise, which is often, perhaps one might even say normally, done to replace expensive workers with cheaper ones.

Given the ethical command, however, it is not right to stop the study at that point. It is necessary to look behind the situation which we are being asked to finance. What is the employment situation in the location which has large numbers of people in the redundancy row, and the other rows in the "terminating relationships" section? What are the local rules and regulations concerning unemployment payments by former employers and unemployment payments by government and local authorities? Has the employer made contributions to a government fund or a local authority fund which is designed to finance exactly this kind of redundancy, and is the fund adequate in size? These questions must all be answered by the finance house before it can arrive at an ethical answer concerning the funding of the project.

Obviously, if there is little unemployment, and if there is a substantial government or local fund for alleviating it, and especially if the employer has been contributing to that fund, there may be no need for any further contributions by the employer. By extension, there need be no further funding sought from the finance house, nor need the finance house feel any need to exert pressure on the client. If the answers to these questions are in the opposite direction, or even if some of them are, the finance house will need to take action to encourage the client to take ethical action, and will need to be prepared to increase the funding for the project by an amount which is big enough to cope with that action.

We have already illustrated how the ethical impact report might be deployed in a plant relocation decision, which was the first of the trial scenarios mentioned in the previous chapter. In the second scenario, that of a corporate merger, the situation is almost identical in the way in which an ethical impact report would be prepared and used. When two companies come together, there are very frequently opportunities for the "rationalisation of operations". This is merger-speak for staffing reductions and plant closures. In quite a few instances, the only real justification for the merger is the fact that the two companies are doing nearly the same things to make nearly the same products, and that there is a substantial cost saving to be achieved if one of them stopped, perhaps with added volume being generated by the continuing one. The economic rationale for business marriages is very commonly of this form.

If this is the situation, we have a need for the same kind of analysis as we discussed under the heading of the plant relocation. The same analysis form could be used, and the same kinds of followup questions could be put. If it were to be found that there was going to be a temporary disruption, but no prolonged loss of livelihood, then no action need be taken. If a serious loss of the probability of gaining a livelihood is inevitable, given the situation in the area surrounding the plant being considered for closure, then the ethical financial institution is under an obligation to insist that its client make restitution, and it must be prepared to raise the necessary additional funds from shareholders or lenders as the case may be.

The shareholding institutions, many of which are pension funds, are commonly believed to be managed by specialist companies who are very nervous of losing the management contract, and who are therefore continually in search of a few pence of extra earnings. They may well not be very keen on having funds allocated toward an ethical objective, which is likely to diminish the return on investment. The pensioners they are supposed to be serving, however, might have a very different opinion. It seems to me highly likely that a group of pensioners and workers (who are potential pensioners, of course) of one company would be very sympathetic indeed to the plight of the workers of another company. They never know when something very similar might be affecting them, after all. The crucial missing element in the chain is that these pensioners, who ought, one might think, to have some say in what is being done with the funds in their name, are never asked what they want to happen. It is all done by the trustees, and the pensioners never even know the question has arisen. Mechanically speaking, this is the single most important link in the process, and that link lies permanently broken under present procedures.

Once the fund managers get the message that the pensioners they are indirectly working for want the fund managed profitably but ethically, it will be very easy for them to change the way they do their appraisals. The fund managers would not find it difficult to add the kind of appraisal discussed above to the exercises they already perform to evaluate a funding request. They just need a bit of help to absorb the message that they will not get fired for being ethical, even if costs a little.

The third of the scenarios was the purchase or sale of a put or call option. These instruments can be used to change the holder's exposure to financial risk in almost any direction and to almost any extent. In normal circumstances, they are the cheapest and usually quickest way to invest in a new theme or idea, provided the companies which are involved in the new topic are big enough to be considered by the option markets.

There are no employment consequences which arise directly from the decision to buy an option. A bad decision may, of course, result in unemployment for the trader who bought the wrong thing at the wrong moment, but that is not really what we have been discussing under the heading of employment consequences.

The way in which option trading can have ethical dangers lies on the option-writing side. The company which makes up the option document is called the "writer" of the option. They are the ones who will have to supply the share to the owner of a call option at the striking price on the expiry date, no matter what it costs them to buy it in the market. On the put side, they are the ones who will have to make the purchase of a share from the option owner, at the striking price, even if they could buy the share for a tiny fraction of that striking price on the open market. The writers are taking on an open-ended commitment in exchange for a small fee, which is determined by a well-specified formula rather than by the action or will of the writer. If the option is naked, which means that the writer does not have the share in stock when he writes a call option, or does not have a call written partially to cover him when he writes a put, the writing of an option is the equivalent of signing a blank cheque.

Individuals who write naked options are either extremely rich, extremely stupid, or behaving unethically. The liability they take on by writing the option is of indeterminate immensity, and, obviously, they are relying on the very considerable probability that they will not have to pay out. The fact of the matter is that they risk bankruptcy with every option they write. The very rich can legitimately take that chance, because they have a cushion of wealth that will protect them from almost any eventuality. The very stupid do not understand what they are doing, and cannot therefore be held to be immoral. There are, however, a few option writers around who quite deliberately write options they know they cannot meet, and rely on a substantial series of wins to generate the funds they would need for their first loss. These people are ready to make a run for it if they should chance to be unlucky enough to be called on the first play.

A more important class of ethical issue arises when a major insurance company writes the options. In many cases, they have a policy of only writing covered options, in which they have the share in stock before they write a call option on it, or in which they cover a put writing with a call at a price which limits their possible loss. No harm in this, it may be quite a useful earner for them. Sometimes, however, these big companies do not take this precaution. They rely on their own sheer size to ensure that they do not suffer irreparable loss, and to ensure that they do not become unable to make the contractual payments on their pension fund liabilities or insurance liabilities.

The regulators vary rather seriously, in my view, on the caution they display on this matter. It seems to me to be a violation of the motto, in that major insurance companies who make a substantial foray into the option writing area are taking a significant risk of depriving some of their pensioners of a livelihood. Further, these insurers will not be able to provide compensation if it were required. Insurers obviously try to downplay this, saying they are covered a hundred times over for these liabilities. I regret to have to report that, in my opinion, in the case of a small number of smaller insurance companies, this is simply untrue. An ethical impact statement in this situation should be designed to ensure that the risk being taken by the insurer was at a level below some generally perceived risk level. The crucial variable would be the probability that a payment on a pension would have to be deferred. This can be calculated, using the volatility of the portfolio of each fund or of each institution, including the options written as an offsetting component of that portfolio. The standard to be used in deciding how much of a risk to take might be drawn up by the regulators or might be adopted by custom and practice within the industry. If a probability of payment deferral of one in a hundred thousand were to be adopted, some insurers would have to change their policies. At a probability of one in ten thousand, it is unlikely that anyone would have to change.

Ethical Impact Reports (2) A Comparison with Environmental Impact Reports.

There is, however, another important issue relating to ethical impact statements which must be covered. This is an argument from analogy, and therefore well known to be unstable. However, there are quite marked parallels between ethical impact statements and environmental impact statements, and it would be helpful to consider this analogy at least briefly. I had been hoping to obtain a lot of useful guidance on how to design an ethical impact statement from the extensive literature on how to do an environmental one, but this was a disappointed hope.

The environmental impact statements are quite unbelievably bureaucratic and regulation-ridden. The earliest of the books consulted was Corwin et al [1975] and this approached the concept of environmental impact statements with a certain amount of idealistic fervour, but even back then in 1975 there was a heavy overlay of California legalism. Senate Document 97 was an important early [1962] document on environmental protection. This document required any water resource project to be accompanied by a document which would "present a comprehensive public viewpoint of the project, including consideration of all effects, beneficial and adverse, short range and long range, tangible and intangible, that may be expected to accrue to all persons and groups within the zone of influence of the proposed resource use" [Corwin, 1975, 23].

This Senate Document also required the presenters of a proposal to list and discuss all the possible alternatives to the project, even if these alternatives were outside the scope of the powers of the agency making the proposal. In bureaucratic terms, this was pretty revolutionary. The idea of the Department of Natural Resources saying they could do a better or cheaper job of providing a particular water resource if the Department of Defense were to shut down a fort might seem like commonsense to some outsiders, but to 1962 civil servants it was almost a declaration of war. The subsequent National Environmental Policy Act of 1969, however, carried the same concept further still. Corwin et al suggest that the effect of this act was to add a sentence to every piece of legislation that had ever been passed by Congress in the two centuries since it began. The sentence might be written as "You (naming the government department or agency) will consider the effect on the environment of everything that we in Congress have authorised you to do". They go on to point out that the legislation has the further effect of forcing the departments to consider all "reasonable alternatives" to what they are proposing to do. The legal fights this legislation has generated are very numerous.

In the UK also, the whole concept of protecting the environment before and during construction projects has become a legal battlefield. The Town and Country Planning Regulations (of various years) obviously have a clear mission of balancing the need to protect and the need to cope with growth of both the population and the economy. The consequence is that the regulations are now the result of arcane arguments about the exact meaning of the terms employed in the discussions on environmental topics.

The team at Oxford Brookes University have made a very thorough study of the whole concept of environmental impact statements, and they have brought out a series of books on the subject. See, for instance, Glasson et al 1994, and Morris & Therivel 1995. These are course books for students who will be fighting the next few rounds of battles between economic development and environmental protection. I do not challenge the accuracy of the Oxford Brookes volumes, but I do find them very depressing. The emphasis of the debate, these texts regretfully report, has moved away from the goal of protecting the environment towards the important secondary goal of writing the environmental impact statement so that the project will pass. It must be clearly emphasised that the Oxford Brookes team remain, as far as one can tell, very committed to the environmental topic; however, they clearly, and I am sure, correctly, feel it is necessary for them to give guidance to their students on the current state of thinking on what will constitute an acceptable application. They discuss the apparent oscillations in the official viewpoint on the matter. The welfare of the environment has, it would seem, become a bureaucratic football.

There can be little doubt that the surge of interest in environmental issues in the last thirty years has improved the overall situation considerably. Perhaps the legal approach, embedded in the UK in legislation such as the Town and Country Planning Regulations, is the best way to continue this progress for the environmental issues. I have to admit that I very much doubt, now, that this approach will work well for ethical issues.

In environmental discussions, there is relatively little doubt that having a lot of diesel fumes is worse than having a small amount of diesel fumes. It is also possible to work out, in a reasonably scientific way, how much diesel pollution is equivalent to a given amount of coal dust. In ethical matters, there is no scientific foundation for the equivalent tradeoffs. The judges would be obliged to make judgements without expert assistance, and we have powerful historical evidence of the difficulty of making ethical judgements consistent. At a minimum, I think we need to try another approach in addition to the ethical impact statement, if that statement is to have a chance of avoiding the fate of its enviromental counterpart.

We have now studied four of the six tools for implementing the second ethical motto, and it is time to pause and update the diagram.

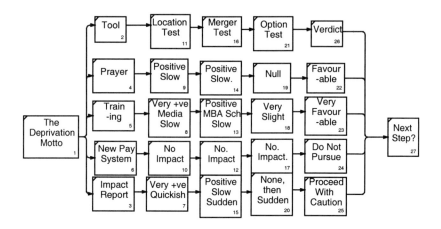

The new payment system is not very promising. It has been classified as having little or no effect, and to be most unlikely to be put into operation. The impact report, on the other hand, has the potential to be a very powerful tool, provided it is handled with great care, so that it does not suffer the fate of the environmental impact report. It is also possible that the impact report could work well in association with the other two promising tools. The impact report could be an element of the training process, and a valuable one. It could also assist religious believers in focussing their intercessions in a concrete way.

New Financial Instruments

This possible solution is an attempt to address the issue of communitarian behaviour directly in a financial context. In this solution the hope would be to structure the capital of the company so that there was less conflict among the capital providers. We are not dealing with retail financial instruments in this section. The tool, in this case, will be a new kind of company share. This tool is quite different from the others, in the sense that it is not an approach to achieving the acceptance of one of the mottoes, but instead is a tool for bringing as many as possible of the stakeholders in a company into a single community. In particular, it is designed to avoid the antipathy which always exists between lenders to the company and everybody else in times of travail.

The specific securities that we are discussing here are those which appear in the balance sheet of a typical business on the liabilities side. This list may include any or all of ordinary shares, preferred shares, debentures, loans, and overdrafts. There are several other items which appear on that side of the balance sheet, but they are not usually securities in the sense in which that term is customarily employed. Shares, debentures and loans are normally documented contracts which specify the rights of their owners and which state the nominal value of the owner's contribution to the total capital of the firm. The overdraft is slightly different, in that it is a loan which varies in amount by the day, and is limited in size only by the overdraft agreement limit. For a large proportion of smaller British companies, however, the overdraft is a major source of capital, and we must consider it in this section. Small American companies have similar needs, and these are met in large measure by periodic loans, which do not vary from day to day, but which fill a role very similar to the role of the overdraft in the capital structure of the firm.

The problem which arises in connection with the existing range of financial instruments is the absence of communitarianism they entail. When the business is prospering, there is no problem at all. The bankers are delighted because their loan is more secure, and the shareholders are delighted because they are richer. When the business enters a difficult patch, however, the community of interest ceases. Not instantly, but steadily as the difficulties mount. The typical loan contract, and certainly the normal regulations governing corporate administration, receivership, and liquidation, give the lenders first right to any assets when the company ceases to trade. The directors are not allowed to continue to trade if they know, or ought to have known, that the company is insolvent. This is not an easy judgement to make, but the duty to make it is clear enough in the rules. This means that the interests of the lenders and interests of the shareholders diverge almost totally. The lenders want to shut down the company the day before its net assets fall below their loan balance. The shareholders want to continue to trade while awaiting an upturn in the market which will enable the lenders and the shareholders to be satisfactorily compensated.   The employees are, generally speaking, on the shareholders side on this point, but they have no real say in what happens.

Debt, as a generality, is always designed to avoid the creation of a community. The lender is seeking to maintain a distance from the company to which he has lent. The relationship is even called "arms-length".   There are good reasons for creating this kind of relationship, of course. These have already been dealt with in the chapter on reconciling the religions' views on disputed topics. Being able to invest in a reasonably safe fashion, for a defined period of time, without having to monitor what is going on in detail, and with a fixed but satisfactory return, is an attraction for quite a few people. The process brings out a lot of investable money from under the mattress, and economic growth happens which otherwise would not.

At the same time, I think it is provable that the legal system is providing a quite ridiculously high level of security for the creditors, at a serious cost to the community at large. The excessive amount of that protection was very well demonstrated by Drexel Burnham Lambert, and especially by Michael Millken, who created a whole industry out of loans that were not as thoroughly protected as the norm. The world of finance knew, perfectly well, once Millken had pointed it out to them, that there was no need for that level of protection at all.

I am not suggesting we should abolish debt; it has been proved worth having in reasonable quantities. I do suggest, however, that there is room for a security which is more at one with the community made up of the shareholders, the workers, and the managers of the enterprise. After having tried out an array of complex and occasionally contorted ideas, I have settled on something really quite simple, which is a close relative of what we have now. It is called a redeemable ordinary share. In the USA it would probably be called a redeemable common stock. It is legally possible to create these items now, but they are very definitely oddities or at least exceptions. I am suggesting they should be regarded as totally routine, and I would hope they would grow to replace half of the total of corporate debt in due course.

A redeemable ordinary share would behave exactly like any other ordinary share with one exception to be discussed below. The share would be issued to buyers at the price which the company's (non-redeemable) ordinary shares were trading for on the exchange. They would be bought in from holders at the quoted price of the ordinary shares on the day of redemption. The dividend paid to ordinary shares would be paid to redeemable ordinary shares, with the same date of record. The tax deductions would be the same. The holders of the ordinary shares would have one vote per share at a general meeting, and the redeemable ordinary share holders would have one vote per share as well.

The difference, of course, is that the ordinary shares would be permanent, and could only be redeemed after passing a special resolution, the quantity to be redeemed limited as a proportion of the total, and supervised by the law to protect the creditors. The redeemable ordinary shares would move in an out as the finances of the firm required them.

For the purposes of computing the security of debt, they would count as debt, and would provide no debt cover. The objective, of course, is that the existence of the redeemable ordinary shares will reduce the amount of debt in issue.

At predefined intervals, perhaps twice a year, the directors would declare an amount of cash they were willing to use for share redemption. The holders of redeemable ordinaries could declare, at any time, that they wanted some or all of their shares redeemed. The smaller of the two totals would be put into operation. On the half-year date, the share price for the non-redeemables would be divided into the directors' cash amount to give the number of shares they could redeem. If this was larger than the number tendered, all the redemptions requested would be made. If smaller, the shareholders would receive a prorata redemption.

A small high tech company (which might be considered highly hazardous, financially speaking) would be expected to issue a lot of ordinary shares and a lot of redeemable ordinary shares and no debt. The original entrepreneurs would probably want to hold on to the ordinary shares, while the venture capital firms and the banks and others with a more fleeting involvement would want the redeemables. They would, however, all have the same interests. When the situation went sour for a while, there would be nobody who could pull the rug on the venture without losing his own investment.

A large financial institution will normally seek to have a broad portfolio balance on both sides of the balance sheet. If it were to be engaged as an investor in redeemable ordinary shares, which it would be obliged to do as the demand for debt capital was reduced, then it would be quite likely to want to issue some redeemable ordinary shares of its own. If the bank was in a good condition, so that the price/earnings ratio was fairly high, the redeemable ordinaries would be a very cheap way for the bank to finance itself. It would not replace debt, in the case of a bank, but it would be a useful additional source of capital. There are new regulations governing the amounts of various kinds of capital a bank must have in place. There is no space in this book to deal with the several technical points raised by this idea, but I suspect that redeemable ordinaries could be classified as "tier one" capital if the bank regulator was able to set or to limit the directors redemption amount.

The new instruments which might be brought into being, and it must be emphasised that a redeemable ordinary is just one of many possibles, could have the effect of making the corporate entity more durable. A heavily indebted company can very easily and quickly go under during a bad period. The interest burden does not have to remain above the profits for long before the bankers want to shut it down while there is still something to sell that might cover the loan. They have no interest in its survival at this stage. They do not share in its profits if it does well. All they want is their interest payments and the capital repayment at the end, and that is what the proprietors have contracted to give them. The proprietors having violated that contract, the creditors have no obligations to keep the venture going. They are not part of that community.

It must be made quite clear that the creditors are not to be regarded as villains because of this. They entered into a contract under which they would perform certain actions, the borrower would perform certain actions, and certain consequences would follow if either side failed to deliver. There is no presumption that any community exists. This is the reason for proposing new financial instruments, and redeemable ordinary shares in particular. Issuing them instead of debt instruments would create a community of interests. This community, consisting of the various kinds of shareholders, would still be in conflict or potential conflict with a range of other groups, including competitors, workers, suppliers, and customers. At least, though, they would not be in conflict with each other about the most basic of business questions:- "should this firm continue to exist or not?".

Given that modest and basic common interest, they would, given poor results, be likely to continue the firm for a reasonable period, until it recovered or until it became obvious that it was not going to succeed. The lender would shut it down far earlier, at a time when the assets just covered the loans. The employees, of course, have no say in this topic according to the law. If the business collapses, they will be out of work. Further, if the shareholders are the only suppliers of capital, there may not be enough money for redundancy payments when the end comes.

Nonetheless, the increased communitarianism involved in this proposed tool, a capital structure that is debt free, would contribute to the achievement of the command concerning the maintenance of probability of livelihoods in a significant and important number of cases. These would be the cases in which, at present, the lenders move too hastily from receivership to liquidation, omitting the option of administration altogether, and close the company down. It is often the case (with hindsight) that they realise they should have waited, but the existing debt-laden capital structure made the lenders too fearful to take that chance.

Law

The idea of trying to enforce ethical behaviour by passing a law is not new. Mencius wrote on the futility of the concept in about 320BC. The problem is that the law is not really enforceable. If the command is "Be Good", the governor or king has the problem of working out what standard to apply. If he insists upon saintly behaviour, he will have almost his whole population in jail. If he selects an arbitrary multi-dimensional description of the good, he condemns himself and others to endless disputation over tradeoffs, for a particular person, between a good score on looking after aged relatives versus a rotten score on road rage. The lawyers would doubtless enjoy it, but the majority would find it quite unacceptable. It is true that society is moving in this direction. I refuse, however, to encourage more of it by recommending this approach. As a general rule, the law has stated that persons are deemed to be good unless they have been demonstrably bad, to an extent which can be established and which can be shown to exceed a societal norm.

If we wanted to use the law as a means of promoting ethical behaviour, we would have to take cognisance of this characteristic. We would not be able to say that people had to be (positively) ethical, only that, if they behaved in certain specific ways, they would be deemed to be unethical, and this would in turn call down a penalty upon them.

We found two ethical commands in the second part of this book, one positive and one negative. It would clearly not be possible to use law to enforce the positive ethical command we derived from the religions. "You have committed an offence if you fail to invent a means of financing the efficient distribution of food to the poorest parts of the poorest nations". Who would "you" be in this sentence? If the invention has not been forthcoming, it is difficult to see exactly who could be left out of prison. If the statement were weakened so that the offence was one of "failing to try to invent a means of financing.. ....", then all we would do, at best, would be to induce the world's financiers to waste a few minutes each year dutifully ticking boxes on a form.

The negative command is easier to implement by legal means. It prohibited anyone from financing a project which would have the consequence of depriving anyone of the probability of earning a livelihood without also financing an adequate compensation scheme. The lawyers would have a field day with this one as well. It would take quite a few court cases to work out what constituted causation of deprivation. More cases to establish what "probability of earning a livelihood" means, and what method of assessing this was to be adopted. More cases still to work out what characteristics a compensation scheme would have to exhibit before it could be deemed adequate. And so on. There is little likelihood that we would ever reach a stable state in terms of the meaning of the law, unless it was drawn up with incredible precision at the outset, which might (and very probably would) have the result that it worked well for a few years and then became unworkable, as circumstances evolved.

It is possible that we will never be able to enforce financial ethical principles unless we put legal teeth behind them. It may be that the villainous and the indifferent, the opportunistic and the selfish, and especially the ordinary finance house employee who is under the gun to produce a good result for the quarter, will ignore all the items that they are not legally forced to consider. Perhaps that is where we will finish, but I would like to try some other methods at the start. Otherwise we are liable to find that ethics has mutated from being a search for something desirable into a bureaucratic obstacle course in the path of economic progress that costs more to operate than it would have cost to provide the compensation sought.

If a legal tool were to be employed, however, it is reasonably clear that it could be effective. There might well need to be a series of court cases to bring out the precise meaning of the negative motto, as suggested above. Alternatively, the British approach of more precise legislation might be used, with no appeal to the courts except in the event of prosecution. In the latter case, an ethical impact report might be required, a possible form of which was discussed in an earlier section of this chapter under that title. This might be required to show backup evidence on unemployment rates and livelihood probabilities in the affected areas, which might in turn have to be endorsed by the auditors of the local authorities responsible for the locations which were being vacated. If these unemployment rates were high, so that the probabilities of future livelihood were low, a cash compensation payment would be required as part of the financing of the move. Arrangements for depositing these funds might involve their deposit with the local authority entity responsible for paying unemployment benefit, or perhaps might involve direct payment to the employees involved. It certainly could be done. At the same time, it would also be a very easy law to evade.

We have now completed our study of the six tools. Let us now update the diagram for the last time, and review the tools for potential effectiveness. The fifth tool, the new redeemable share, does not fit into this framework and has been left out. It seems to be a promising tool, however, and should be pursued further.

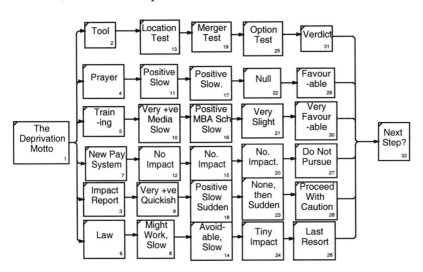

The conclusion of this chapter seems to be that the most promising route forward would be to employ several of the tools. The impact statement would work well in conjunction with prayer and with training, and would almost certainly have to be a feature of the legal solution if we found ourselves forced to adopt that last resort. It seems unlikely to work very well on its own, however. The environmental impact statement saga, in which attempts to use impact statements on their own very rapidly degenerated into a very messy legal muddle, should be a warning against use of ethical impact statements without the support of some other tool.

The balance of probabilities of success therefore leads us to the suggestion that all those in favour of the general mission of this book should [1] employ redeemable ordinary shares, and [2] employ impact statements in conjunction with training and mind expansion, and further that religious believers who are in favour of the mission should [3] employ impact statements in conjunction with intercession.

Chapter 12:- Consequences and Conclusions

In chapter one, and especially in diagram two in that chapter, the pressures which were being exerted upon capital market workers were described. These pressures were seen to operate in a closed loop, so that the demands made by each party for better results led to increased pressure on the next entity in the chain, and eventually led to more pressure on the party which started the process. The circular motion has the effect of causing the pressure to build slowly but surely over time.

The call for "shareholder value" by journalists, economists, finance professors, and politicians claiming to speak on behalf of pensioners, employees, and other beneficiaries has put pressure on trustees of funds. Fund trustees have pushed the financial institutions to do better. The institutions have demanded more from the fund managers. The fund managers have "leaned" on the banks and the big companies. The big companies have leaned on the banks and the little companies and their employees. The banks have become stricter about their relationships with big companies, little companies, and employee households. The concerns of the households have been heard by the journalists and the politicians, and the entire cycle restarts.

It is appropriate at this stage in the book to consider whether what we have been discussing will help to solve this problem, or make it worse, or leave it pretty much as it was before.

We have sought guidance from four of the religions, and have concluded that they instruct us to behave in a range of specific ways, most of which we have been doing, in the capital markets and in other areas of business, for a considerable period. We have also identified two specific orders from the religions, which we have not been doing, or at least have not being doing well enough. These tasks remain in front of those of us who work in the capital markets, as unfinished ethical business, and demand our attention. The first was the problem of financing the provision of food and other essentials to the poorest parts of the poorest nations. The second was the need to finance a "lifebelt" for those people and those communities which would otherwise lose all prospect of making a living because of some feature of a project we are funding.

The first task, as was mentioned in chapter nine, has started to receive attention. The New York meeting in June 1998 has not fixed the problem, but has made a very promising beginning. The approach being taken is to facilitate the establishment of numerous micro-lending institutions, and to link them into the international capital market system. There is a lot to do, in terms of strengthening the micro-lenders and improving the information flows, but at least a start has been made on the issue. The presumption is that these micro-lenders will devote a large proportion of their energies to the problems of third world food production, food quality, and food distribution. Certainly, that is what they have been concentrating on up to now.

We have discussed the second issue at considerable length in chapter eleven, and have considered a range of ways in which it might be implemented. We concluded that three of these solutions ought to be pursued, and that one was especially promising. This involved training and "mind expansion" in conjunction with "ethical impact statements". Readers who have skipped directly to the conclusions chapter are going to have to back up, at least to chapter eleven, for an explanation of these terms. It is safe to say, however, that the time spent on training or on mind expansion would lengthen the training period of capital market workers, while the time taken to prepare an ethical impact statement would lengthen the period required for the scrutiny of a financing project. Is this time investment worthwhile?

The judgement as to whether it is worthwhile for capital markets workers to understand the ethical consequences of their actions must always be a subjective matter. Some would argue, as a matter of course, that everyone should understand the ethical consequences of their actions, whether they are capital market workers, journalists, bus drivers, or professors. Others might argue, in the case of capital market workers, that the ethical consequences of the actions of people to whom these capital market workers have supplied funds should not be regarded as a matter of concern to the capital market workers. The argument of this book opposes that view with vigour.

There is a spectrum of ethicality. The financing of a heroin shipment would probably be illegal even if the financier did not know that was what he was assisting, and must be clearly unethical even if the financier managed to escape legal sanction. The financing of a merger for which the only rationale is cost reduction is completely legal, but can cause as much community damage as the heroin shipment in certain situations. A significant minority of these transactions would be clearly unethical even though they break no law, for reasons discussed in chapters ten and eleven. The financier in these cases, who claimed that his investee's actions were nothing to do with him, is building his defence on moral quicksand.   At the other end of the spectrum, of course, are the millions of transactions which are clearly ethical, whether legal or not.

This kind of debate could go on forever without a binding conclusion. It seems better to avoid these rather subjective arguments and fall back on the arguments from enlightened self-interest. Let us take another look at diagram two, and think about what is going on.   The pressure is building. It has been building for at least twenty years.   There is no force at work which is stopping the pressure from becoming greater.   It is not possible to predict which element of the system will collapse under the strain, and it is certainly not possible to predict when that collapse will come.

At the moment, we might use the analogy of an old-fashioned steam engine without a safety valve; it might explode in a minute, or it might explode in an hour, but as long as we keep stoking coal into the burner we can be sure it will explode sometime.

Eventually, somewhere, some community is going to declare the pressure from the capital markets to be intolerable.   Other oppressed communities will join in.   These communities may be in third world countries, but are rather more likely to be the deprived areas of the richer countries.   In July of 1998, the auto workers of Flint Michigan, a stronghold of both the General Motors Corporation and of the United Auto Workers union, were on strike. Loud voices were being raised in complaint that the company was making cars in Mexico and bringing them into the USA. It is places like Flint where the losses have been felt most acutely. It is obviously not possible to say exactly what the outcome of such a complaint will be, but it can be expected to be the more severe, the longer we let the pressure build.

Would it not be better, perhaps even safer, to build in a safety valve? My answer to that question is a definite "yes". In a physical system, a safety valve is relatively easy. Put a fusebox in the electrical circuit. Insert a low pressure valve in a system of steam piping. They will do their job by failing before the rest of the system is in danger. In a human system, however, the approach must be different.   We do not want the human system to stop; we just want it to change direction by a moderate amount.

The law is not really a very good instrument for persuading managers in companies, whether financial or industrial, to strengthen themselves in ethical terms. Law deals with uncertain but rather rigid boundaries between "legal" and "not legal". All the lawyers can do is to move onto the moral battlefield after the ethical struggle is at an end, and bayonet those of the morally wounded whose failings were most manifest. We do not really need that sort of negative incentive; we need a positive one, or several of them.

The objective of such a positive incentive approach would be to increase the number of dimensions of performance of a company, with particular reference to a financial services company. If the company is regarded solely as a producer of dividends and capital gains, then it might as well ignore all ethical considerations which are not enforced by law. If, instead, it is regarded as a producer or wealth which also has systems in place that ensure quality, avoid pollution, and enforce ethicality, then the business seems, almost as a matter of definition, to be on a higher plane. What needs to be achieved to is create ways of assessing such achievements, and then to educate the entities in the diagram two loop to applaud attainments on all of these dimensions. We let the "steam"out of the system by educating the entities to understand that there are several dimensions of progress and improvement, and that a given investment company or a given bank may well choose, in certain years, to make most of its effort in one of the dimensions that is not purely cash.

As a general rule, companies do not receive any applause or congratulations when they behave well. This is not surprising:- behaving well is, after all, the normal way of behaving. At the same time, it is true that companies do change their behaviour in response to favourable public recognition. In the UK, the Queen's Awards to Industry were greeted, at their time of introduction, with contemptuous cynicism by the reporters of the day, but they have since had a major effect. They are now so firmly recognised that British companies which want to do business in Japan are finding that they have some explaining to do if they have not been granted one of these Awards.

In a similar fashion, the Malcolm Baldridge Awards are issued by the Department of Commerce in the USA to recognise up to six companies a year for their excellence in terms of product, process, or service quality. The criteria for the prize are deliberately loose, and allow each company to demonstrate in its own way how its systems and procedures are designed and developed to make sure that the output is as perfect as possible.

We do not, at present, have a system for rewarding ethical behaviour by means of prizes, and I am not sure it would be a good idea to create such a system. However, it would be perfectly possible, and I suspect desirable, to create a system of rewarding, or at least recognising, the ethical preparedness of those companies which have formal systems and procedures in place to make sure that ethical issues are taken properly into consideration at all relevant stages of the managerial process.

A significant ethical achievement should be the subject of congratulations and public applause. Creating systems which make sure that people have to give thought to ethics when taking all major business decisions would indeed qualify as significant ethical achievements.

I am not suggesting that we should give a prize to a company for a single manifestly ethical action. Johnson and Johnson's $100 million recall of Tylenol would clearly be deserving of any such prize. A lunatic poisoned some of their medicines in a store, and seven people died. The company recalled ALL the Tylenol, to eliminate the risk of further deaths, at great cost to themselves. Fortunately, there were no further deaths or injuries. J&J gained immense respect by this action. However, I would not think it sensible to give an award or prize for that action. It is too random. Instead, the company might be rewarded for having in place the corporate procedures which were able to produce the ethical result quickly.

The objective of the book was to see what we could learn from the religions about the ethics of finance. In doing this, the goal has been to identify commands from the religions which we have been obeying, ones we are starting to obey, and ones we have not yet begun to obey. It is beyond the scope of this book to write out the exact details of how all the proposals should be implemented. The idea of an award for companies which have systems which enforce thinking about ethical issues, in particular, would require another book, and the co-operation of several large foundations, banks, and major businesses. At the same time, I hope the book has succeeded in showing how the thoughtful study of financial ethics may enhance the status of the financial community in the medium to long term, even if it may add a little to our collective workload in the short. The epilogue which follows is offered as this author's personal agenda for making progress. I hope some other people

151

may feel interested enough to join in this effort, or even to take over some of the job. It is a big task: I hope readers will have agreed, by now, with my conclusion, which is that this task is worth doing.

Chapter 13:- Epilogue:- An Action Plan

There are quite a number of leads which have been identified in the previous chapters which are crying out for action, and I am very conscious that I cannot pursue all of them. This short chapter is a "shopping list" of work that needs to be done, and is written in the hope that some readers will identify one of more elements as being areas where they could help and would like to do so.

First of all, ethical command one is completely outside my own area of expertise. I know almost nothing about food distribution, and food distribution in the poorest parts of the poorest countries is even more of a closed book to me than other parts of that complex industry. Fortunately, a lot of conscientious and well-intentioned people who know a lot about this problem have tried to deal with it, but claim to have met with only partial success. Several of the units of the UN have been working on this for decades, and have achieved considerable success, while leaving a lot still for the future. I was therefore delighted and more than a little relieved to learn of the work that is being done at the Washington and New York conference to link the micro-lending institutions to the capital markets. It can be assumed safely that food distribution lending will be one of the major product lines of these tiny banks. They have made it clear that there is a great deal to be done, but the major financial institutions involved have the matter in hand and work is progressing. Perhaps more importantly, with the lessons of the Grameen Bank and its few imitators before us, the people who are the potential beneficiaries of this programme may be persuaded to contribute their only resource, time, to the furtherance of the work.

The second item on the shopping list is the concept of the redeemable ordinary share. I am reasonably certain that this will be a very useful idea for bankers of the Islamic world. It would be a method whereby they could make investments in the corporations of the western world, if they so wished, without violating the instructions of the Quran. These shares would also be of great interest to the entrepreneurial managers of the small and medium sized enterprises of western countries, who would welcome investors on this basis. The objective, in this instance, is not really one of getting Islamic finance into western companies, but to initiate the use of redeemable ordinary shares in western countries. If enough of these companies employ the idea, then western banking firms will start to offer them as well, to avoid losing market share. If the plan works well, the redeemable ordinary share may take over a substantial amount of that portion of the corporate financing market currently held by debt. It was pointed out in chapter eleven that, for certain kinds of companies, debt is morally and therefore practically the wrong kind of capital for them to issue, and that its reduction as a proportion of the total capital would be desirable. The task in this instance would be to act as a broker between an Islamic bank of some size and a British or American development capital firm to get the whole thing started.. At the same time, it should be possible to make some headway on this second item on the shopping list by inviting the interest of one or more of the British merchant banking firms which are active in middle eastern financial affairs. These firms could expect to make some brokerage income from the development of this concept, so it may well make rather more rapid progress than some of the other suggestions put forward in this book.

The third item on the shopping list would be the combined effect of an ethical impact statement and prayer. This could obviously be undertaken by any believer on his or her own initiative. To develop the concept to a fuller form, however, it would be necessary to engage the bureaucracies of the churches, synagogues, and mosques to carry it forward with an approximately united voice. My previous experience with this process has not been favourable. There are other people who are certainly going to be better than I will ever be at getting theological officialdom to move. I hope to persuade the Finance and Ethics forum or some other similar groups to identify the best people to be approached, and the best people to do the approaching. The power of this approach is very great, potentially. The four religions account for nearly four billion people, between them, and there only are six billion altogether. I would regard this approach as potentially very important, so it must be tackled from the right angles, with the right pace, and with the right approach. This will take care and time, and certainly will need additional inputs from people who are more "theologically correct" than I.

The fourth shopping list element is the combination of the ethical impact statement with the training and educational process. This will be a slow process, but it certainly should be pursued. I hope I can contribute to the task of pursuing it. There are dozens of courses happening in British universities every term dealing with capital investment appraisal and with mergers and acquisitions. Typically, the seven or eight class sessions allocated to this topic will be devoted to the mathematics involved, and to studying the four most common ways of doing the sums. A bit of time is also spent on the tricky problem of estimating the cost of capital, and some spend time also on the problems of risk and uncertainty and how to handle these topics in a capital spending context. I offer no criticism for the inclusion of these topics in the course. I take considerable exception to the fact that the students do not receive any instruction about the community impact of what is being proposed, and do not receive guidance on how to handle the concerns of the disrupted towns or counties or nations they are affecting. The entire computation is phrased in simple economic terms, and the "answer" depends on whether the net present value is positive or negative.

It would not be appropriate for me to complain that finance teachers did not use my second ethical command, as that has only just become available in its present form. It would not, however, be unjust to complain about their continuing emphasis on the numbers and their inadequate attention to the moral and other qualitative issues. I have to confess to having been guilty of the same omission in prior years. This is an omission which could be repaired, over a ten year period, reasonably easily. It would require strong advocacy at conferences attended by the people who write finance text books, and it would require some effort on a consultancy basis to get the corporate finance manuals to reflect the additional factors to be considered. This would all take time, of course. I would hope that I could make a bit of headway on this part of the problem by personal intervention. More importantly, I would hope to be able to assist others who become interested in financial ethics so that they will be able to continue the effort of effecting procedural changes of the appropriate kind in the corporate office and in the MBA classrooms. It can be done. It will be slow.

At least I can report that a start has been made. I offered a course to honours students taking the Bachelor of Commerce at Edinburgh University in early 1998. Sixteen of the honours year of about a hundred and twenty chose to take it, and the results were extremely pleasing. They learned a lot about how to think ethically on financial matters, and I learned a lot about what works well as I try to help them gain familiarity with this new and different field. The second offering in the spring of 1999 gave me further insight into the training task.

Discussions are in progress concerning how best to progress this educational effort. Three institutions have expressed an interest in having a course on Financial Ethics taught, and one has expressed an interest in carrying the work forward to the next generation, probably through the vehicle of a small-to-medium scale doctoral programme offering. There is a lot to be done. A start has been made.

The fifth and last Action Plan item is the inauguration of the Ethical Systems Standard. This would be a matter of drawing up a programme, analogous to that used in the Baldridge awards for quality, which would allow a company to demonstrate that it had well-designed and effective systems in place for making sure that ethical issues are considered at all relevant times in the management process. I hope to approach a substantial supranational enterprise in the financial field to see if they would be interested in the establishment of an award. I would hope that it would be a matter of demonstrating the presence of systems, so that quite a large number of companies could meet the standard at the same time, in much the same way as the Queen's Awards work. The Baldridge method is very sound, but seems too restrictive with a maximum of six winners a year.

I have not copyrighted or patented the above work list! Others who would like to seize a portion of it for themselves are entirely welcome to do so. There is more than enough to keep everyone who is likely to be interested busy for years.

Bibliography

Ali, M.M. (1973) *The Holy Quran*, 6th edn. Chicago, USA: Specialty Promotions.

Allah (1964) *The Koran*, Oxford: Oxford University Press.

Asquith, P. (1983) Merger Bids, Uncertainty, and Stockholder Returns. *Journal of Financial Economics* **11** (2):51-83. Nederland: Elsevier Science.

Bentham, J. (1787) Defence of Usury. 1st edn, New York: Theodore Foster,1838.

Bentham, J. (1843) Of Imprisonment for Debt. In: Lester, V.M. (Ed.) *Victorian Insolvency*, pp. 44-55. Oxford, UK: Clarendon Press]

Birch, B.C. and Rasmussen, L.L. (1989) *Bible and Ethics in the Christian Life*, 2nd edn. Minneapolis, MN USA: Augsburg Fortress.

Bishops, A.C. (1986) *Economic Justice for All*, Washington DC: US Catholic Conference.

Black, F. and Scholes, M. (1973) The Pricing of Options and Corporate Liabilities. *Journal of Political Economy* **81** 637-654. Chicago: Univ Press Chicago.

Bowes, P. (1977) *The Hindu Religious Tradition:- A Philosophical Approach*, London: Routledge & Kegan Paul.

Brealey, R.A., Myers, S.C., and Marcus A.J. (1999) *Fundamentals of Corporate Finance*, 2nd international edn. London: McGraw Hill.

Corwin, R., Heffernan, P.H., Johnston, R.A., Remy, M., Roberts, J.A. and Tyler, D.B. (1975) *Environmental Impact Assessment*, San Francisco: Freeman Cooper & Co.

Dharmatrata and Sparham, G. (1986) *The Tibetan Dhammapada*, 2nd edn. Delhi: Mahayana Publications.

Falk, N. A. (1990) Stories of the Great Donors. In: Sizemore, R.F. and Swearer, D.K. (Eds.) *Ethics, Wealth, and Salvation. A Study in Buddhist Social Ethics*, pp. 215-234. Columbia, SC, USA: University of South Carolina

Fowler, K. (1979) The Ethics of Instalment Credit. In: Hopps, R. (Ed.) *Ethics in the World of Finance*, pp. 24-45. London: Chester House]

Friedman, M. and Friedman, R. (1984) *Tyranny of the Status Quo*, London: Secker Warburg.

Glasson, J., Therivel, R. and Chadwick, A. (1994) *Introduction to Environmental Impact Assessment*, London: UCL Ltd.

Goldziher, I. (1910) *Introduction to Islamic Theology and Law*, Princeton, NJ, USA: Princeton University Press.

Holcombe, S. (1995) *Managing to Empower:- The Grameen Bank's Experience of Poverty Alleviation*, London: Zed Books.

Hopkins, E.W. (1924) *Ethics of India*, New Haven: Yale Univ.

Hume, R.E. (1931) *The Thirteen Principal Upanishads*, 2nd edn. Delhi: Oxford Univ Press.

Innes, W.C. (1983) *Social Concern in Calvin's Geneva*, Allison Park, PA, USA: Pickwick Publications.

Jochim, C. (1980) Ethical Analysis of an Ancient Debate:- Moists versus Confucians. *Journal of Religious Ethics* **8** (1):135-147. Knoxville, TE, USA: Univ of Tennessee.

Kassis, H.E. (1983) *A Concordance of the Qur'an*, Berkeley,CA, USA: Univ California Press.

Katz, J. (1989) *The "Shabbes Goy" : A Study in Halakhic Flexibility*, Philadelphia: Jewish Publication Society.

Kerr, S. (1975) On the Folly of Rewarding A while Hoping for B. *Academy of Management Journal* **18** (4):769-783. Mississippi StateUniv: Academy of Mgt.

King Jr, M.L. (1986) Letter from Birmingham City Jail. In: Washington, J.M. (Ed.) *A Testament of Hope:- Essential Writings of MLK Jr*, pp. 289-302. San Francisco, CA, USA: Harper & Row]

Luke, R.H. (1979) A Christian Approach to Compromise. In: Hopps, R. (Ed.) *Ethics in the World of Finance*, pp. 82-87. London: Chester House Publications]

Maimonides and Rabinowitz [trans], J.J. (1949) *The Code of Maimonides: Book 13: The Book of Civil Laws*, New Haven, Conn, USA: Yale Univ Press.

Maimonides, M. and Peppercorne (trans), J.W. (1840) Alms and the Collector, and the duty to contribute. In: Anonymous *The Law of the Hebrews relating to the Poor and Stranger*, pp. 57-63. London: Pelham Richardson

Mencius (1932) *Mencius*, New York: Longmans Green.

Moles, P. and Terry, N. (1997) *The Handbook of International Financial Terms*, Oxford: Oxford Univ Press.

Montgomery Watt, W. (1962) *Islamic Philosophy and Theology*, Edinburgh: Edinburgh University Press.

Montgomery Watt, W. (1979) *What is Islam?* 2nd edn. London: Longman.

Morris, P. and Therivel, R. (1995) *Methods of Environmental Impact Assessment*, London: UCL Press Ltd.

Northcott, M., Plant, R., Forrester, D.B., Sykes, S.W., Loades, A. and Lash, N. (1991) *Vision and Prophecy:-The Tasks of Social Theology Today*, Edinburgh: Centre for Theol and Pub Issues.

Peters, T.J. and Waterman, R.H. (1982) *In Search of Excellence,* New York, Harper and Row

Preston, R. (1987) Is there a Christian Ethic of Finance? In: Anonymous *Finance and Ethics: Occasional Paper Number 11*, pp. 1-13. Edinburgh: New College

Preston, R., Shaw, J., Elliott, C., Alexander, K. and Jenkins, D.E. (1987) *Finance and Ethics*, Edinburgh: Centre for Theol and Public Issues.

Quasem, M.A. (1975) *The Ethics of al-Ghazali*, Kuala Lumpur: Author.

Raffer, K. (1990) Applying Chapter 9 Insolvency to International Debts: An Economically Efficient Solution with a Human Face. *World Development* **18** (2):301-311. Oxford, UK: Pergamon.

Rahula, W.S. (1974) *What the Buddha Taught*, 2nd edn. New York: Grove Press Inc.

Rajavaramuni, P. (1990) Foundations of Buddhist Social Ethics. In: Sizemore, R.F. and Swearer, D.K. (Eds.) *Ethics, Wealth, and Salvation. A Study in Buddhist Social Ethics*, pp. 215-234. Columbia, SC, USA: University of South Carolina

Rasmussen, L.L. (1993) *Moral Fragments and Moral Community:- A Proposal for Church in Society*, Minneapolis: Augsburg Fortress.

Rowley, H.H. (1951) *Submission in Suffering, and other essays on Eastern Thought*, Cardiff: University of Wales Press.

Ruthven, M. (1984) *Islam in the World*, New York: Oxford University Press.

Schubeck, T.L. (1993) *Liberation Ethics*, Minneapolis, USA: Augsburg Fortress.

Sizemore, R.F. and Swearer, D.K. (1990) Introduction. In: Sizemore, R.F. and Swearer, D.K. (Eds.) *Ethics, Wealth, and Salvation. A Study in Buddhist Social Ethics*, pp. 215-234. Columbia, SC, USA: University of South Carolina]

Smeeding, T.M., Rainwater, L. and Atkinson, A.B. (1995) *The Luxembourg Income Study*, Paris: OECD.

Umaruddin, M. (1962) *The Ethical Philosophy of Al-Ghazzali*, Aligarh: Aligarh Univ.

World Bank (1995a) *Annual Report 1994*, Washington,DC,USA: World Bank.

World Bank (1995b) *The World Bank Atlas 1995*, Washington DC: The World Bank.

INDEX